LATINAS
ON THE LINE

Invisible Information Workers
in Telecommunications

MELISSA VILLA-NICHOLAS

RUTGERS UNIVERSITY PRESS
NEW BRUNSWICK, CAMDEN, AND NEWARK,
NEW JERSEY, AND LONDON

Library of Congress Cataloging-in-Publication Data

Names: Villa-Nicholas, Melissa, author.

Title: Latinas on the line : invisible information workers in telecommunications / Melissa Villa-Nicholas.

Description: New Brunswick : Rutgers University Press, [2022] | Series: Latinidad: transnational cultures in the United States | Includes bibliographical references and index.

Identifiers: LCCN 2021015635 | ISBN 9781978813717 (paperback) | ISBN 9781978813724 (cloth) | ISBN 9781978813731 (epub) | ISBN 9781978813748 (mobi) | ISBN 9781978813755 (pdf)

Subjects: LCSH: Hispanic American women—Employment—United States—History. | Telecommunication—United States—Employees—History.

Classification: LCC HD6072.2.U5 V55 2022 | DDC 331.4/816408968073—dc23

LC record available at https://lccn.loc.gov/2021015635

A British Cataloging-in-Publication record for this book is available from the British Library.

References to internet websites (URLs) were accurate at the time of writing. Neither the author nor Rutgers University Press is responsible for URLs that may have expired or changed since the manuscript was prepared.

♾ The paper used in this publication meets the requirements of the American National Standard for Information Sciences—Permanence of Paper for Printed Library Materials, ANSI Z39.48-1992.

www.rutgersuniversitypress.org

Manufactured in the United States of America

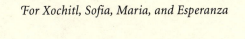
For Xochitl, Sofia, Maria, and Esperanza

CONTENTS

ABBREVIATIONS

AFL	American Federation of Labor
AT&T	American Telephone and Telegraph Company
CRLA	California Rural Legal Assistance
EEOC	Equal Employment Opportunity Commission
FCC	Federal Communications Commission
FEPC	Fair Employment Practices Committee
GTE	General Telephone and Electronics
HSO	Hispanic Support Organization
IBEW	International Brotherhood of Electrical Workers
ICT	Information Communication Technology
IT	Information Technology
MALDEF	Mexican American Legal Defense and Education Fund
NFTW	National Federation of Telephone Workers
NOW	National Organization of Women
PT&T	Pacific Telephone and Telegraph
SCOT	Social Construction of Technology
SMSA	Standard Metropolitan Statistical Areas
STEM	Science, Technology, Engineering, and Mathematics
STS	Science and Technology Studies
WTUL	Women's Telephone Union Local

LATINAS ON THE LINE

INTRODUCTION

Monica, a first-generation Mexican American woman, was eighteen years old when a White man asked her to apply for a job at Southern California's Pacific Bell. She was certain she would fail the many tests required for the position. Indeed, the testing would later prove to have been one of many methods that the Bell system[1] utilized to keep people of color out of employment. But Monica was applying in 1970, when Bell was under investigation by the Equal Employment Opportunity Commission (EEOC) for broad discriminating hiring practices, including this bias-based testing. The Bell system, like many companies of that time period, was hustling to diversify before the federal government stepped in again. Three years later, Bell and the U.S. government would come to an agreement via a consent decree, an affirmative action mandate that opened up the largest private employer to underrepresented people. Amid these changes, Monica earned her first full-time job in telecommunications, along with many Latinas in Southern California and major metropolises around the country.

"I could definitely tell that they were looking for minorities to work there, because everyone there was White, and they had to fill that gap; you could totally see it,"[2] Monica told me. She was initially hired as a telephone operator in the Torrance office. She was paid well, and Pacific Bell also covered the cost of her tuition at community college. She eventually transferred to the El Camino office near LAX, where there was more opportunity to move into different positions. According to Monica, "The higher you went up in the floors, the better the job got. I started in the mail room, and then I went to the fourth floor. There were actually computers there."

After her move to the fourth floor, Monica worked with a decollator, a machine that pulls long rows of carbon paper apart from computer printouts. She took data tapes from the accounting center and transferred the wheels of tapes to a supercomputer. But there was something just as unsatisfying about data entry on the fourth floor as there was about telephone operator work. Monica was not permitted past a large glass window to the supercomputers. She brought the data that processed employee information to the supercomputers but learned that only White technicians could use the computers. "I didn't feel like I accomplished much," she said to me. "I didn't know why I wasn't allowed to go into the big computer center. We weren't allowed to go in there, and I wanted to go in there."

The feeling of separation from sophisticated technologies that Monica expressed was echoed in other Latina information workers' interviews. Though it was not the glass between manual data entry work and the supercomputers that I kept coming back to but a story Monica told me about her time in the mailroom. The mailroom had the lowest pay grade on the bottom floor of Pacific Bell, but it was the most comfortable environment for Monica because she worked with other Latinas and African American women. One day, a White man from one of the top floors

came to the mailroom when I was a mailperson. Out of a White lady, an African American woman, and me, he said to me, "I need you to do this right now." And he had a set of keys and a little tiny key. And he threw a bunch of keys in front of me, sitting down, and he said, "I need you to find the key right now that matches this one." And the African American woman I worked with said to me, "Don't do that. That's wrong, what he's asking you to do." And I was scared. I went ahead and looked for a key, but there was nothing like that. And I really feel like to this day he did that on purpose.

I just felt like he was trying to make a point that I needed to be working. You know, because there were times that we had a lull in the mailroom. And, you know, I just felt that he singled me out, so it was very uncomfortable. Because it was ridiculous, to try to find a key that matched a key. And there were hundreds of them, but no match.

Latinas in telecommunications, information technology, and the larger science, technology, engineering, and mathematics (STEM) workforce have often been made to feel like the matching key Monica was asked to find—nonexistent. Latinas were invited into telecommunications, but there was often no matching space, job title, or technology to make them eligible for full membership into the telecommunications family. Nonetheless, after decades of information labor, it is deeply embedded into their identity, their mobility, and their private lives. Latina information workers live a double reality, where information technology is deeply rooted in their everyday work and practices, yet they are also excluded from more advanced IT fields.

When I was young, the American Telephone and Telegraph Company (AT&T) was a household name, discussed regularly in our day-to-day lives and at the dinner table. For my family, AT&T was not just the landline provider on our 1980s touch-tone phones; Pacific Bell, the California subsidiary of AT&T, was our livelihood. My parents met working in a mailroom at Pacific Bell. When changes in telecommunications were in the news, we watched with an awareness that seemingly everyday shifts in the political economy would deeply impact our everyday lives. An interwoven story between my family and AT&T predated my own life. Part of me always knew that the most infamous telecommunications monopoly in the world was foundational to our lives. But a chapter of the story went unspoken in my family—something not discussed when we worried about labor strikes or closing offices or saw landlines become wireless. A question waited for me in the future: How did most of my aunts and uncles, a first-generation Mexican family who had not yet been to college, end up in various jobs in telecommunications?

It was common to hear stories about the work in AT&T. Little anecdotes about my mom receiving "crank calls" while working the operator's cord board. Or when my uncle, a lineman, had fallen off a telephone pole and broken his arm. I knew that AT&T and my family were intricately connected in an uneasy marriage. But I did not know the *why* and *how*. Why did AT&T hire my family? *Why* did my family stay with or leave this uneasy relationship? *Why* were all the Latinas I knew at one time in their lives connected to the phone company? In mainstream media and politics, Latina/os were discussed in conjunction with immigration, education, "crime," poverty, factories, and migrant farm labor. However, Latinas within telecommunications was not an issue discussed among politicians, unions, or community organizing groups. So *how* did Latinas come to be established in tele-communications, working different parts of a corporate machine that kept telephones ringing and would one day lead us here, to individual internet access through smartphones? This book is a response to a question I asked long ago.

The time period of this critical inquiry into Latina narratives of telecommunications begins in the early 1970s, when the Equal Employment Opportunity Commission, via the Federal Communications Commission (FCC), rejected a request by AT&T to raise their rates (Green, 2001) as a tool to force AT&T to diversify their workforce. Latinas entered lower levels of information technology sectors with the resulting EEOC-AT&T affirmative action consent decree and were "included" into the economic systems of labor at a distance, their difference used by private sectors for expanding capitalism. While such fields as communications and the history of computing have explored in depth AT&T's history, Latinas' accounts from within telecommunications have yet to be written. This research purposefully focuses on Latinas employed in telecommunications for most of their lives, starting in the early 1970s and 1980s, their lives resoundingly impacted by the civil rights movements and subsequent affirmative action laws. The entry of Latinas into telecommunications in the 1970s marked a new path of telecommunications' history, one that takes into account race, gender, sexuality, and culture, all identifiers at play as Latinas have gone to work "on the line."

Although Latinas have often gone "unseen" in technology-based fields, they continue to work in the invisible information labor sectors that fuel the services housed under telecommunications. Today, these women are approaching the end of their careers, having worked for decades in data entry and customer service, as telephone operators and electrical engineers, and in other blue- and white-collar services. There is a dearth of research on Latinas in telecommunications, despite their lifetimes' worth of information technology skills in telecommunications' services and phenomenological knowledge. The histories of Latinas in telecommunications contribute to the larger canons on Latina labor, communications, race, gender, and social constructions of technology. By partnering a mixed-methods approach of archives and oral history, the histories of telecommunications will become strengthened through a heterogeneity of memory.

With telecommunications' archives and Latina oral histories, I conclude by proposing a Latinx technology studies, a method of analysis that acknowledges that Latinas' experiences provide critical insights into the social histories of communications and technologies. Moving toward a Latinx technology studies requires not only that we demand a higher employment rate of Latinas in information technology fields but also that we recognize *where* Latinas are working in the tech industry. Often this means looking away from the visible information technology (IT) jobs and into the unseen sectors of the tech labor force. The invisibility of Latina information labor promulgates the ideology that technology is neutral and uninfluenced by the relations of powers that dictate everyday life. Telling this history moves Latinas out from behind the cord board and acknowledges that major technology conglomerates are not established by "self-made" tech CEOs but rather powered by many people working at different levels of information labor.

Differentially Included in Telecommunications

In telecommunications, Latina information workers began at the end—the end of manual engineering, the end of an imagined White "Bell family," the end of the welfare state in transition to neoliberalism, and the end of old technologies as new technologies emerged. Latinas were recruited into telecommunications during a transitional time, in which the benefits from the previous century were dissolving. From the implementation of divestiture in the 1980s through the heightening of the globalized economy and labor systems, Latina information workers found that the family system they had come to know dissolved over the span of their careers. They entered into information technology sectors differentially included, as Roderick Ferguson (2012) describes the experience of people of color into previously segregated spaces: both necessary and never fully accepted. The effects of this were Latinas who worked in highly surveilled, technologically shifting spaces, with little opportunity to move beyond customer service and blue-collar engineer roles, and who were valued for their potential for Whiteness.

My goal is to demonstrate a fuller picture of a Latina information and technology history in telecommunications, by way of their own narratives. Latina information workers, limited in their mobility in these technology-based fields, both inhabit and reject their belonging to the telecommunications industry. For Latinas, the effect becomes an intimate relationship with telecommunications and information labor that impacts not only their perspective on the liberalizing global economy but also their domestic and personal lives.

Latinas have long been the body, or conduit, for which information technology is delivered. But in telephony, the Latina story also demonstrates how the telephone and its supporting parts act as a bridge for the potential for Latina/o Whiteness; it is able to moderate the characteristics that are not White enough and deliver the parts of *Latinidad* that are desirable to conservative values and the American economy. This emerging theme is what I call the *Latina technological potential*. Telecommunications differentially situates mestizo Latinas for their potential to pass into Whiteness, with technology as the mediator for racial qualities that are marginalized in the United States *and* the use of technology to buffer the "Latino threat," the threat Americans have long expressed around Latina/o presence and nonassimilated identity that Latina/o studies scholar Leo Chavez so aptly named (Chavez, 2013). For example, during my interviews, I noted that those Latinas without an accent were assigned as telephone operators while those with an accent were given other data entry jobs that did not put them in public customer-based visible roles. We will see this trend through the history of Latina/o technological labor as well—that Latina/os are at times acceptable information workers *at the exclusion of* another information laborer.

This inquiry into Latina narratives of telecommunications begins in the early 1970s, when the Equal Employment Opportunity Commission, via the Federal Communications Commission, rejected a request by AT&T to raise their rates (Green, 2001) as a direct action against AT&T for their discriminating hiring and employment practices. Latinas entered lower levels of information technology sectors with the ruling of the EEOC-AT&T affirmative action consent decree of 1973 and subsequent rulings that impacted the larger telecommunications field and technology-related sectors (Green, 2012). The consent decree was a landmark case between the Department of Justice and the largest private-sector employer (AT&T) and acted to eliminate the discriminatory recruiting, hiring, and promotion practices that worked against women and minorities. The decree led to a large payout of fifteen million dollars to increase the pay of thirty-six thousand women and people of color already working for the company (Green, 2001).

The U.S. economy included Latinas into information labor at a distance, their difference used by private sectors for expanding capitalism. While such fields as communications and the history of computing have explored in depth AT&T's history, and Latina/o, Chicana/o, and labor studies have a wealth of research on Latina labor in the United States, Latinas' accounts from within telecommunications have yet to be explored. This research focuses on Latinas employed in telecommunications for most of their lives, starting in the early 1970s and 1980s, and how they were resoundingly impacted by the civil rights movements and subsequent affirmative action laws of the era. Latina memory of telecommunications and the phone companies, in particular, takes into account race, gender, sexuality, culture, and the deeply embodied experience of the globalizing workforce and neoliberal economic policy—all identifiers in circulation as Latinas have gone to work "on the line," and what would later become online. Leading with Latina insights creates an entrance into the intersecting identities of race, gender, sexuality, and class as coconstructors of technology.

This time period sits at the crux of many shifts in U.S. society, politics, and economics. The 1970s were impacted by the aftermath of the civil rights movements of the 1950s and 1960s, affecting increased legislation on affirmative action in the workplace (Padilla, 1997). Although women and men of color and White women were integrated further into various blue- and white-collar employment, the economic structure of the United States began to change, with the previous manufacturing industries broken down or sent overseas, the defunding of the public sector and increased government support of the private sectors, and the flourishing of new economic industries such as information technologies (Harvey, 2011). For Latinas, the 1970s were prefaced by a wave of Chicano rights movements with different goals to improve the quality of life for Latina/os in the United States (Martinez, 2010). But Latinas often found themselves at an uneasy intersection of movements between Chicano rights, often male dominated, and the feminist movement, usually associated with White women's rights. These movements, though creating social change, often relegated Latinas to the periphery of identity politics.

A turn in manual labor toward information labor came with the "information age" when, in the 1960s and 1970s, "knowledge was supplanting capital and labor as the decisive factor of production" (Schiller, 2011, p. 6). Latina information workers can span across industries depending on their labor. Traditional forms of Latina labor are valued and represented in fields such as migrant work, domestic work, and the retail industry. However, with the commodification of information, Latinas are found in various sectors doing "information work," working with various information technologies and often in the role of information service—such as being telephone operators or working customer service—in roles that are between white and blue collar, sometimes "pink" collar, reserved for women, but often in the customer service industry where gender and feminization are utilized as a tool to "soothe" customers. These service workers have been strategically positioned in informational blue- and pink-collar fields for their front-facing work meant to appease customers through feminization, but because of race and ethnicity, their rights as workers and vertical mobility into more sophisticated work with technologies is capped to information service professions (Villa-Nicholas, 2016; Green, 2001).

While AT&T's history and the case between the *EEOC v. AT&T* mostly took place on the East Coast, California has played an important role in Latina history, citizenship, and labor rights, and was the epicenter for hearings and legislation against Pacific Telephone and Telegraph (PT&T), the California Bell company owned by AT&T. The Chicano rights movement inspired the formation of such California rights groups as the Mexican American Legal Defense and Education Fund (MALDEF) and the California Rural Legal Assistance (CRLA), both involved in the *EEOC v. AT&T* case. With large communities of Latina/o populations and a history of Latina/o foundations, California is a source of political forces and inspiration for Latina rights in the United States.

Latinas continue to work in the invisible information labor sectors that fuel the services housed under telecommunications, with lifetimes' worth of information technology skills. These histories can contribute to the larger canon on Latina labor, communications, race, gender, and social constructions of technology. Latina perspectives and histories offer a unique entrance into the history of telecommunications because of their experience with the globalizing and liberalizing economy and the cultural impacts of their identities and labor. They engage in what Cara Wallis (2013) calls "socio-techno practices," in which they both incorporate and reject the narratives of telecommunications, technology as progress, and the greater shifts in the national and global political economies.

The Latina experience is also critical to understanding the contemporary information economy and digital age. The women interviewed in this book are approaching the end of their careers, having worked for decades in data entry, customer service, telephone operation, electrical engineering, and other blue- and white-collar services. They entered the largest telecommunications company at a time when information labor was increasingly becoming automated. From the ground level of information labor, they experienced technological automation, the shifting economy, AT&T divestiture, the dot-com bubble and the burst of the dot-com bubble, and the reorganization of the economy and society around the internet and mobile technologies.

Early in the conversation on the histories of underrepresented peoples in computing was Venus Green's (2011) work on race, gender, and Whiteness in the telephone company. Green braids infrastructure, technological development and evolution, corporate development, labor, and customer engagement to give a fully comprehensive history of the Bell system and how it intentionally gendered the development of the operator cord board and further dehumanized working conditions as it was required to employ more people of color. Green finds that the telephony technology was intentionally developed to minimize laborers such as the telephone operator, not because they were less efficient, but because they demanded better working conditions and better wages.

Mar Hicks (2017) pulls back the curtain of computing and reveals that women in Great Britain were the early computing workforce. As Great Britain automated their work and boasted a technological revolution, tech labor became further gendered, and previous woman laborers in that workforce were weeded out, their knowledge and skills lost and leaving a noticeable gap that hindered the sophistication of technological innovation. The creation of the internet in the United States has traditionally been told as that of a military project, the work siphoned off into military personnel. Joy Rankin's (2018) work demonstrates that indeed the public was engaged in the early development of the internet, through programs in public universities across the country. The internet as we know it today was developed by many users' engagements, such as university students (Rankin, 2018), rather than just the Silicon Valley elite or lone figure hackers. It was also developed by taxpayer funds, so it not only wasn't the invention of a mythical lone White male figure but was also invested into by Latina/os, who paid for it thrice: as taxpayers, as laborers, and as consumers.

Infrastructure and information labor are also a part of this bigger picture of invisible information labor, and there are many scholars that describe the inner workings of our digital lives and the people behind the labor of our internet access. One example of this is YouTube. Algorithms cannot catch the greatest of atrocities uploaded to the internet, and so information workers must screen red flag content and determine if it should be removed. Sarah Roberts names these workers as *commercial content moderators*, "professional people paid to screen content uploaded to the internet's social media sites on behalf of the firms that solicit user participation" (2019, p. 1). Those commercial content moderators suffer debilitating mental and physical conditions as a result; however, due to their invisible role and the nature of their work, internet users rarely know about their presence. Mary Gray and Siddharth Suri name the many people that work in businesses such as Facebook, Instagram, Twitter, and Amazon as *ghost workers*, those information workers that work in the lowest rungs of these high tech and multibillion-dollar industries. These workers may be located all over the world, intentionally invisible but working as the backbone of "AI." "As builders create systems to transfer tasks from humans to machines, they surface new problems to solve through automation" (Gray and Suri, 2019, p. xxi), however, that automation, in turn, leads to new problems where ghost workers must troubleshoot.

There are many information laborers at different levels of these major tech conglomerates, and not all are counted as highly paid "STEM" employees or working in the famous luxury conditions of the Google and Facebook campuses. Diverse groups of people that are bemoaned for their lack of representation in the valued sectors of STEM are delivery drivers for Amazon Prime packages and work in Amazon packaging facilities, notorious for their exploited conditions (Sainato, 2019). Another example is the manufacturers of smartphones and the deadly labor conditions under which they are assembled. The most famous example is the iPhone manufacturer Foxconn, located in Longhua, China. Over ninety-nine million employees assemble iPhones in highly skilled and low-paid working conditions, which have led to notoriously high suicide rates at the plant (Sohail, 2020). The raw materials that it takes to build a smartphone are also a lucrative and deadline business, the mining of which takes place in the Democratic Republic of the Congo, which supplies 60 percent of the world's cobalt. Apple, Microsoft, Tesla, and Google all have investments in the cheap mining of cobalt, which has led to children's and adult's deaths who work in those mines (Ochab, 2020).

Latina/os in STEM

This analysis is especially timely given the increasing demand in the United States for Latina/os to be recruited and retained into technology-related fields. Recent revelations from large technology conglomerates reveal that Latinas are overwhelmingly underrepresented in science, technology, engineering, and math (STEM) industries (Burnett et al., 2009). With the release of diversity statistics by the major technology corporations of Silicon Valley—such as Google, where Latinas make up just 1 percent of employees (Google Diversity, 2013)—diversity advocacy groups are now calling for more visibility of Latinas in STEM fields. *Scientific American* writer Mónica I. Feliú-Mójer (2014) asserts, "The underrepresentation of Latinas in STEM is detrimental to the advancement of science and innovation, and to society," arguing that advocacy from within places of privilege changes the field. Some have pointed to the need for a shift in education for Latinas, who comprise a total of 7 percent of the STEM workforce (Caballero, 2014). The absence of Latinas in Silicon Valley, STEM, and IT fields has reached national awareness in popular media (Bohorquez, 2014).

Although the demand for Latina/os in STEM is particularly urgent, it is crucial to acknowledge those who have already been working in the lower level sectors of STEM industries—the telephone operators, data processors, electrical engineers, and invisible information workers who deploy critical skills that allow these industries to flourish. While these statistics do warrant immediate attention, it is important to note that many Latinas have worked in information technology sectors for most of their lives. Though rarely reaching white-collar positions within telecommunications, Latinas have indeed worked in the blue-collar sector that propels technology to the center of the global economy today (Villa-Nicholas, 2014).

METHOD

The invisibility of Latina information labor also promulgates the ideology that technology is neutral and uninfluenced by the relations of powers that dictate everyday life. Latina labor is often found among the most tedious jobs that are meant to be invisible while allowing technology to run smoothly; call centers, data entry, and customer service all function to assist the appearance that information technologies run autonomously, without human support. Telling this history moves Latinas out from behind the cord board and acknowledges that major technology conglomerates are not established by "self-made" CEOs (as they are so often presented) but rather powered by many men and women working at different levels of information labor.

Focusing on the impact and reflection of being both included and excluded in information labor and various parts of the technology sector, I look at Latinas' everyday work in telecommunications coupled with their reflections on years of labor. I analyze how Latinas are not only intricately enmeshed in the information labor sector of the U.S. workforce but also personally reflective on having lived through decades of a liberalizing economy and globalized workforce. Latina information laborers have been included in the U.S. narrative of citizenship through affirmative action but also experience dissonance at their embedded and embodied experience of the impact of neoliberal policy on their everyday work.

My method examines and interprets Latina memories of telecommunications, information and technology labor, and the shifting economy from 1970 to 2013 and then builds the history of the developments of telephony, telecommunications, and the phone company around those memories. I interviewed Latinas *first* and then dove into the MALDEF and CRLA archives at the Stanford University archives. I explore multiple discourses that arose from oral history interviews and archival texts: the deeply personal experience of telecommunications by Latinas, the constantly changing information technology sector, the shifting identity formations and narratives in reflection of the liberalizing economy in Latinas' personal and public lives, a reflection on transnational (un)belonging, and the discourse around being Latina in a recently integrated and evolving field. I attempt to engage fully the decades of embodied experience that Latinas have had as telephone operators, telephone engineers, customer service operators, data entry technicians, and internet customer service specialists.

I engage the oral history narratives of Latinas in the telecommunications workforce in Southern California who began their work as a result of the 1973 affirmative action consent decree and have just recently retired in the early 2000s. I examine how these women remember telecommunications and information labor, how their identity and subject formations are intimately engaged with information technology and the globalizing labor force, and how information technology labor and culture became intertwined in their public and private lives.

This project embraces the personal experiences expressed in my oral history interviews. Latinas bring to telecommunications a unique perspective due to their cultural, gender, racial, ethnic, regional, and linguistic differences. Latina histories in telecommunications will not only broaden relevant fields of study but also offer valuable insights into previously overlooked AT&T accounts.

I approach my research collaborators as both autonomous individuals with their own unique identities, autonomy, and agency and also people who are subjects of their surroundings. Subjectivity acknowledges the preexisting conditions that situate Latinas in telecommunications (Rodríguez, 2003, p. 5). Subjectivity and identity are not easily separated, often existing within the same discursive spaces. But using subjectivity can neglect Latinas' own way of being, situating them in a world that only organizes them and does not allow them to shape their own ways of knowing (Rodríguez, 2003, p. 5). Identity practices allow for agency. Juana María Rodríguez advocates that "the challenge becomes how to conceptualize subjectivity through both semiotic structures (discursive spaces) and agency (identity practices) by investigating the ways these fields work to constitute, inform, and transform one another. Discursive spaces exist at the site of knowledge production" (Rodríguez, 2003, p. 5).

Among my research subjects in the archive and collaborators of oral history, identities vary by many factors, such as region, nationality, culture, language, and experience. Identities are not fixed but rather in a constant state of production and reflection (Oboler, 2002, p. 85). Identity is the Latina self, placed into telecommunications and all the spaces that came before, with "preexisting narratives" (Rodríguez, 2003, p. 5). When thinking about the coconstruction of Latina subjectivity, telecommunications, and technology, those preexisting narratives of each factor organize Latina identity. Through these socially constructed identities that are always at play (gender, class, age, race, place), telecommunications and Latinas become intertwined, "which in turn reproduce[s] and restructure[s] these identities" (Wallis, 2013, p. 4).

Intersectional identities, telecommunications, information technologies, and the larger information economy engage with visible and invisible systems of power. Intersectionality, as identified by legal scholar Kimberlé Crenshaw, is a lens with which to view multiple oppressions experienced in identity (1989). Crenshaw used a Black feminist framework to encourage the intersection of racism and gender. Patricia Hill Collins later extended these intersections to her metaphor of a matrix of domination, in which she adds multiple layers of race, gender, class, sexuality, nationalism, and age (2011). Without this intersectional understanding, we are left with an inadequate analysis of the history of telecommunications, the ways in which Latinas analyze information technologies, and the contemporary implications of Latinas in information technologies with a historical perspective.

INVISIBLE INFORMATION LABOR

Latina identity is both always in process and also a marker of their difference in a previously all-Anglo space: "Cultural identities come from somewhere, have histories. But, like everything which is historical, they undergo constant transformation" (Hall, 1990, p. 225). Identity differences in these spaces of power are enclosed into hegemony. Power is enforced, negotiated, and acted upon on macro levels, such as the state and institutions, and from below, between subjects of the state for whom biopower benefits or works against. Latina difference is not only positioned at odds with the larger "norms" of telecommunications but also used to recirculate and make possible the hegemony of the larger institutions.

Technology-centered sectors such as telecommunications have historically marginalized groups such as White women, women and men of color, sexual minorities, and nonbinary people. Recent scholarship has encouraged documenting the historical existence of these marginalized people into the histories of computing and information technologies (Hicks, 2017; Rankin, 2018). New media and feminist scholars challenge that the goal is not solely to "write" underrepresented people into the history of technology but also to interrogate the racial and gendered formations of power that organize information technology work (Wajcman, 2009; Fouché, 2012). Information technologies do not have a value-free context but rather politically influence and construct their timelines (Winner, 1986; Noble, 2018). Latina information workers are already applying these critical engagements to their quotidian labor, challenging value-free assumptions about information technologies. They do this by such actions as not paying their bills online, not subscribing to an ideology that technological change always equals growth and progress, and naming the inequality in their workplaces.

Part of my goal is to promote the recruitment of more Latinas to higher-ranking positions in STEM-related fields, which is directly linked to promoting social justice in the form of labor, gender, and race equality. Therefore, Latinas, historically marginalized within STEM academic fields and labor, use a critical framework to balance the historiography of information technologies and resist neutral approaches to research.

The study of Latina information workers lags within the history of computing, science and technology studies (STS), new media studies, the information sciences, Latina/o studies, and women's history. This work is especially situated within studies of labor and production. Latina/o labor is a part of U.S. labor history. As Latinas become an increasingly visible part of the population in the United States and STEM fields further diversify their workforces, Latinas' histories in IT fields are more urgent. This research extends the understanding of histories of technologies and telecommunications more generally and deepens the knowledge of Latina sociotechno histories.

PERSONAL POSITIONING

My personal background informs this investigation. I am a Latina, a first-generation college student who benefits from White privilege. My family came into the working middle class by way of telecommunications, having found jobs in the field during the 1970s after the monumental consent decree. Being raised in this culture, I have long been immersed in the personal stories, physical structures, and everyday interconnection of information technology work, and have seen firsthand how it plays into the public and private lives of Latinas. Therefore, this research is deeply personal and resists narratives of "objectivity" or neutrality that eclipse STEM fields. Just as my theoretical framework acknowledges the social constructions of everyday life, I recognize that my own epistemological background impacts my approach to research—how I collect, interact with, and analyze data.

I began this research conducting interviews in the summer of 2013 and have been following through with interviews and archival research in the preceding years. This book is not a deep dive into the history of telecommunications, which has been chronicled successfully by many scholars.[3] It is also not a history of technology wherein I demonstrate a shift in technology affected by Latinas. This approach centers Latinas first and tells the story of telecommunications and technology second. As the fields of STS, the history of computing, and critical information sciences continue to flourish, we must continue to reorganize with women of color as the leads of these stories. White women and women of color have long been the backbone of invisible labor in information technology sectors (Nakamura, 2014). Bringing them to the front of the story will not only provide new insights into a long-told tale but also *improve* the conditions in which they work, the ways in which technology is designed, and the social impacts that those technologies have (Hicks, 2017; Green, 2001). In my seven years of research, writing, rewriting, and reflecting on these histories, I have also come to the conclusion that these women have invaluable insights into their decades of experience that cannot be reproduced or found in the archive or in large data sets. Thus I reach back into the well of what communities of color and ethnic studies scholars have long argued: that prioritizing oral histories and storytelling from underrepresented people draws on undeniable and indispensable knowledge that cannot be found in mainstream archives or canonical narratives.

TERMINOLOGY

I use the word *Latina* as an imperfect term that homogenizes a diverse group of women, and the term *Latina/o* as a describer of the larger group of people who live in the United States by way of Mexico and Central and South America. By choosing *Latina*, I have also made a choice not to use *Hispanic* and *Chicana* to label my interview participants and the women engaged during the *EEOC v. AT&T* case. The term *Hispanic* has been contested because of its connection to colonialism and imperial politics. *Hispanic* in the United States was first used by "wealthy descendants of Spaniards from New Mexico and other Mexican territories, recently acquired in the U.S. in the late nineteenth century" (Cruz-Janzen, 2002, p. 159). Marta Cruz-Janzen argues that *Hispanic* was a term used to align Spaniards with American Whites, rather than with Indians and Mexicans, referring directly to Spanish origins (2002, p. 159). *Hispanic* has also been typically associated with U.S. census terminology, which homogenized a population of people from Spanish-speaking countries despite their diverse backgrounds in nationality, linguistics, culture, politics, race, religion, and gender (Oboler, 2002, p. 77).

Denise A. Segura and Beatriz M. Pesquera (1998) define Chicanas as women of Mexican heritage in the United States. Chicana feminists were early organizers, artists, teachers, scholars, and writers who sought equal treatment regardless of race, class, and gender. Chicanas frequently experienced discrimination due to their race, ethnicity, and gender in education, jobs, and politics. *Chicana* was an identifier that signified not just ethnicity and race but also political movements for intersectional rights. I use the term *Chicana* or *Chicana/os* in the following chapters only when it relates directly to Chicano rights movements. Although my interview collaborators did not identify as Chicana, I acknowledge the term as a significant political movement to Latinas in the present day.

Many in the field of Latina/o studies have criticized the all-encompassing term *Latino* for homogenizing a wide array of people from different ethnicities, cultural traditions, languages, and nation-alities. However, Marysol Asencio describes the preference for the term *Latina/o*: "As such, some prefer the term Latino since they believe the unifying thread is more about the social and political relation-ship within the U.S. context than cultural similarities deriving from Spanish colonization . . . the term Latino is used to refer to Caribbean and Latin American heritages while sometimes excluding Spain, a European country, and including Brazil as a Latin American country" (2010, p. 3).

I want to resist a narrative that all Latinas might respond in the same way to their experiences as information workers or navigators of information technologies. I agree with Saldana-Portillo that within Latina/o studies there must be a critical scholarship and a "critical consciousness of empire . . . that is 'tirelessly reckoning with America's past,' but also with its present, through an examination of how dis-placed cultures of racialized immigrants trouble national narratives of democracy and equality" (2007, p. 508). *Latina* is not a neutral or descriptive term; it includes a politically engaged debate about the sta-tus of Latina/os as citizens or immigrants in the United States.

The word *Latina* will further break down when I examine the qualitative narratives of Latinas in telecommunications who do not identify themselves as "Latina." *Latina* is a word I choose for scholarly purposes. However, I want to reject it as an end-all term for this study, which embraces the slippage of signifiers according to how my inter-view subjects construct their own narratives.

The term *Latinx* has recently entered the public and academic sphere as a way to supplement the gendered signifiers of "a/o" in "Latina/o" and to neutralize the gendered identity of "Latina/o" or "Chicana/o" (de Onís, 2017). The term *Latinx* resists gender binaries by including the potential for gender nonconforming outside of the a/o gender binary that signifies female/male. There are many bene-fits to the term *Latinx*, including hailing a diverse community more broadly within the United States and *not* assuming genders while dis-cussing large plural groups of people. I use *Latinx* only when refer-ring to my push for a Latinx technology studies, a critical approach to analyzing information technologies. This research chooses *Latina* as an imperfect label because all the people interviewed identified as cis-gender and women-identifying, with their ethnic background being mostly Mexican. Perhaps because of a generational difference, these Latinas did not identify with the term *Latinx*. Recent research has demonstrated that *Latinx* is a term relegated mostly to the spheres of academia and only used by 3 percent of the larger Latina/o population (Noe-Bustamante et al., 2020). Indeed, all the women I interviewed identified with different terms—including Mexican American, Hispanic, indigenous Mexican, and Latina—demonstrating the heterogeneity and slippage that happens when attempting to group together Latina/os, even those with the same ethnic, occupational, and geographic background.

Organization of the Book

The historical record of this experience works as the site for shifting Latina identities and critical reflections on the neoliberalizing economy and the globalized information labor force. I interview Latinas who worked in Southern California to understand their own narratives and their evolving identities of citizenship, inclusion, and dissonance in a "borderlands" of information labor.

In arranging these chapters, I considered both the telecommunications timeline, starting in the 1970s with the affirmative action consent decree, and the corresponding narratives of identity and reflection of information labor. I begin by discussing the history of telecommunications, information labor, and Latina incorporation in this sector and the shifting political landscape of the neoliberal workforce. This work starts with a wide-angle, panoramic view of Latina/os in information and technology labor and then slowly narrows into a microscopic focus on one Latina's experience in telecommunications.

In chapter 1, I discuss the context of Latinas entering into information and technology labor, reviewing the historical moves that led to the inclusion of previously excluded groups into telecommunications and the broader information technology labor force. In this chapter, I want to give the contextual premise of Latina/os in technology to demonstrate where in the timeline of technological development Latinas in telecommunications lands; I braid Latina/o information technology histories and telecommunications' racial and gendered history, building up to the consent decree as a way of setting the scene for

Latinas recruited into information labor. I also seek to give a bird's-eye view of Latina/o histories of technology, demonstrating that when the literature is brought together, there is indeed already a historical record.

Chapter 2 focuses on the moment of the consent decree and how Latinas were overlooked during this monumental lawsuit. While telecommunications were challenged to diversify, human rights organizations neglected intersectional identity, and Latinas became invisible in the outcome.

Chapter 3 focuses on interviews with Latina information workers in the greater Los Angeles area who have worked for decades in telecommunications, from the 1970s to the present. This chapter argues that Latina information workers' oral histories from the 1970s through the 1980s articulate subject formation and resistance from within telecommunications. Latina identity within telecommunications offers new insights into formations of labor, reflections on digital capitalism, and intense experiences of neoliberal shifts in the political economy.

Chapter 4 looks at the formation of the "Bell family" and Latina inclusion and exclusion from this family. The Bell family concept was built around an antiunion identity formation of Whiteness and gender in the early twentieth century. Latinas entered AT&T just as the company broke down the idea of the Bell family due to shifting gender roles and the inclusion of people of color. However, in interviews with Latina information workers at AT&T, the Bell family was reflected on fondly as a preneoliberal system of inclusion and benefits. The theme around the Bell family brings forth an interesting dynamic of contradiction and reflection on the inclusion of the emerging liberalized political economy.

Chapter 5 follows one Mexican American woman's thirty-year life story as a demonstration of the Latina/o experience in the phone company. This chapter focuses on one subject's experience with telecommunications, the phone company, and technology. This approach resists the narrative that lone White men—such as Steve Jobs, Mark Zuckerberg, or in the case of the Bell system, Theodore Vail—"invented" the modern digital world, a mythology that Joy Rankin (2018) names the "Silicon Valley mythology." My interview with Lorraine demonstrates a way to focus on one story to see a "life cycle" of telecommunications, technology, and the Latina experience.

In the conclusion, I reflect on the bigger picture of Latinas missing in the histories of computing and telecommunications, as it resonates personally and structurally, and advocate for a Latinx technology studies.

A deeper look at telephony, telecommunications, and Latina identity reveals that the telephone and information technologies in telecommunications were utilized as a buffer for the potential of acceptable *Latinidad* in the United States. A Latina telephone operator could "pass" and be imagined as a White woman through the cord board, whereas a Latina/o who spoke Spanish as a telephone operator was limited to *only* speaking Spanish at the cord board, with the telephone serving as a buffer for their non-Westernized cultural attributes. When we look at the ways in which the telephone, telecommunications, and the technology industry developed while engaging Latina/o people, we see that information technology has been valued for its potential to fix the nonassimilated parts of Latina/os.

Latina information workers who persisted in their profession applied a critical perspective to their work and the political economy that organizes and is organized by telecommunications. The implications for such work are clear: Latina experiences in telecommunications offer critical insight into the histories of information technologies that we might not have otherwise.

1

WHY LATINAS?

OVERLAPPING TECHNOLOGY HISTORIES

For decades, researchers, higher education educators, advocacy groups, and the media have brought attention to the dearth of Latina/os in STEM. Two national trends parallel each other: the heavier investment of resources into STEM fields in universities and in industry and the stagnant inclusion of Latina/os in STEM college programs and in higher ranking STEM professions. Year to year, this publicly known problem has been bemoaned, and subsequently research, funding, and programming have aimed to bridge the gap between Latina/os and STEM employment. More recently in 2018, a PEW Social Trends poll found that Latina/os made up 16 percent of the U.S. workforce but only 7 percent of STEM workers and were 6 percent of the STEM employed workforce with a bachelor's degree or higher (Funk and Parker, 2018). Researchers have found that the lack of representation of Latina/os in STEM is rooted in the barriers that Latina/os face in higher education. However, Latina/os in the United States and along the U.S.-Mexico borderlands have always been present in the development of technologies and in STEM fields and industry, albeit in less visible roles. This chapter seeks to contextualize the history of Latina/os in technology-related fields.

Traditional conversations of interrogating the intersectional frameworks around ICTs have occurred in disciplinary silos. Within the broader field of media and communication, Latina feminist media studies (LFMS) has called on traditional feminist media studies to bring the focus of Latinas out of the margins and understand that the Latina body is the surface on which media are imprinted (Cepeda, 2016). Although LFMS has decades of scholarship exploring Latina/o media use, representation, and circuits of culture (Valdivia, 2018), it has often relegated information and communication technologies (ICTs) as another "form" of media rather than as the primary function from which media are now launched. Fields that center the critical technological analyses, such as the history of computing, science and technology studies, and critical information sciences, tend to relegate the study of Latinas and technology as a marginalized and infrequently discussed subgroup of users (de la Peña, 2010) rather than centering Latinas. But within the history of computing, LFMS media studies, and Latina/o studies, we can find a well-rounded story of the history of Latina/o use, creation, consumption, and production of information technologies.

Latina/os are interpellated by and engage with information technologies, interrogating new media as "both a liberatory resource and a troublesome entity in need of constant surveillance and self-discipline" (Cepeda, 2016). Ultimately, we see a similar engagement with older and new media: they reflect that Latina/o users both express agency by way of that technology and are also subject to the ways in which power is circulated with that technology. When brought together, the fields of media and communication studies, Latina/o studies, and the history of computing create a rich patchwork of the Latina/o histories of technologies.

The following chapter lays out various overlapping histories to provide a foundation for Latinas entering telecommunications and telephony: first, a Latina/o history of technology; second, a raced and gendered evolution of the phone company—two chronological histories in two parts that merge when Latinas enter into telecommunications, as detailed further in chapter 2.

Latina/os as Technological Conduit

Latinas have been invisible laborers in telecommunications and information technologies for decades. Indeed, the history of Latina/os in the United States is worthy of review to understand: *Why these women? Why this time?* What we find in reviewing the past few centuries of

Latina/o technological labor is that the Latina/o body has been *the surface on which information technology is mobilized.*

Mainstream narratives around Latina/os often focus on a lack: a lack of Latina/os in STEM or a lack of Latina/os who have information and technology literacy. Visual representations of Latina/os in the United States portray a people without a technology—domestic and culinary laborers who largely work manually. But Latina/os do have a history of labor with emerging technologies in the United States, and it has often been rendered invisible. When Latina/os are visibly associated with information technologies, it is to serve the function of Western capitalism. Between those dichotomies, the narrative of Latina/os who actually work with, interact with, create, or disrupt information technologies is *the most valuable tool that can resist technological hegemony.*

The Latina/o technological potential is demonstrated throughout Latina/o technology histories, as the Latina/o body is cast as biologically suited to manufacture information communication technologies in borderlands. Contemporary forms of digital labor reveal that Latina/o digital representation and digital labor is not isolated or a new phenomenon but rather has been building since the Treaty of Guadalupe Hidalgo, when many Mexican regions joined the United States. Latina/o technological labor is often the conduit by which technology is delivered to U.S. consumers, and the Latina/o body is increasingly the body around which digital technology is designed. Latina/os have long worked in the underbelly of the technological industry and have been immersed in the development of information technologies for decades. However, Latina/os have often been part of the invisible information labor of STEM or in the development of information communication technologies, while also challenging the politics of technological development, demonstrating that "looking inside digital culture means both looking back in time to the roots of the computing industry and the specific material production practices that positioned race and gender as commodities in electronic factories" (Nakamura, 2014, p. 937).

As we continue to see more technology built around the surveillance of the Latina/o body, we can look at Latina/o technology laborers of the past to see some of the common ties. I argue that the Latina/o body, throughout history, acts as the slate upon which information technology is inscribed and that Latina/os inscribe and change information technologies themselves. Latina/os have also been active consumers with information and communication technologies, exercising their agency in challenging hegemony through use.

THE NINETEENTH TO TWENTIETH CENTURIES

The life cycle of AT&T and other telephone companies has long been intertwined with the growing Latina/o population in California, and not by coincidence. Westward expansion occurred by way of the Mexican-American war from 1846 to 1848, justified through Anglo racial superiority and the ideology of Manifest Destiny. After the Treaty of Guadalupe Hidalgo and the annexation of Mexico, the United States developed westward through the emerging technologies of the railroad, the telegraph lines, and the telephone lines. Those technologies are symbiotic: the telephone lines followed the railroad track as the station operator was also the telegraph operator (Garcílazo, 2016, p. 13).[1] Indeed, Bell's first long-distance call was about the U.S.-Mexico border: a discussion on March 7, 1916, between attendees at a Bell banquet in Washington, D.C., and General John Pershing, who was located in El Paso, on the border of Mexico, and proclaimed in the phone call, "All's quiet on the border" (Wu, 2011, p. 4).

Mexican men were recruited to build new technologies of the time—like the railroad—from 1870 to 1930, and this set the precedent for Latina/o digital labor and Latina/os' value as a necessary part of building technologies. Railroad labor was previously performed by Irish, Chinese, and Black men in the 1800s. Mexican labor increased in the early nineteenth and twentieth centuries due to the Chinese Exclusion Act and the exclusion of Black men in labor (Garcílazo, 2016). A common theme that emerges throughout Latina/o technological labor history is the switch between Asian information labor and that of Latin Americans, and Mexicans in particular. There is a cycle of intolerance for foreigners from the Western gaze, especially when it comes to information technology labor, and Asian—especially Chinese and Indian—labor is often in rotation with Latina/o labor.

Mexican men were labeled as "semiskilled" and as "common labor," typical descriptors applied to Latina/o information and technology labor, as they built the railroads in the southwest and central plains. They were subcontracted by labor agencies and not directly employed by telecommunications companies, which is a pattern that reemerged with neoliberalism and the shifting labor landscape Latinas in telecommunications experienced during their lifetimes. These men were known as *traqueros*, which refers to Mexican or Mexican American railroad track workers (Garcílazo, 2016). The Mexican male body was often described in terms of a superhuman ability to work, particularly compatible with the landscape of the western United States. Mexican men's labor was also closely aligned with "bringing" Manifest Destiny by building the railroad: "In the minds of most Euro Americans, their victory over Mexico reinforced the notion of white supremacy and Manifest Destiny. This conquest opened the Southwest to the United States technology and markets, which in turn made Mexican labor in the newly conquered lands available for appropriation" (Garcílazo, 2016, p. 13). The image entitled *American Progress*, John Gast's painting on Manifest Destiny, depicts these narratives of Whiteness and colonization as the train and the telephone lines move westward into what was formerly Mexico and colonized Native American territories.

A 1912 edition of the *Railway Age Gazette* notes, "The Mexican is an interesting type of track laborer, and one with whom the average roadmaster or supervisor is unfamiliar. Five years ago his activities in this country were confined to a limited area in the southwest adjacent to El Paso and the Mexican border. Within the past three or four years Mexicans have been in such demand and have come into this country in such numbers that they are now the main source of supply for the roads west and south of Kansas City and are found in large numbers in Missouri, Iowa and Illinois" (McHenry County Historical Society and Museum, n.d.). Mexican men's bodies were objectified as superhuman in order to bring this new technology across the country and interpellated as a product necessary for the assemblage of the train in the United States. Mexican men in particular became associated with the efficiency and superstrength of the train itself, and not only in the Southwest.

In the context of Latinas in telecommunications, we learn from the *traqueros* that from early on, Mexican labor and the Mexican body in the United States became the avenue through which technology arrived. The Latina body began to become publicly associated with technologies as factories moved out of urban midwestern cities, such as Detroit, and into *maquiladoras*, beginning in the 1960s. This developed an early link between industrialization and the trade of wages for a technological labor process based on Latina labor. Jefferson Cowie notes that "by analogy, the Mexican plants assembled clothing and electronics for U.S. corporations and charged a fee in the form of wages in return" (2001, p. 113). The Radio Corporation of America (RCA) moved down to the U.S.-Mexico border in the 1960s, where Mexican women's labor in the borderlands would produce the over-whelming majority of electronics that circulate globally.

Maquiladoras led to a gendered division of labor, as *maquiladoras* sought to hire women—specifically young, unmarried women. Similar to their male counterparts, Latinas were presented as biologically suited for the work of electronics production. One Juárez plant manager said in an interview, "They have the gift of fine and delicate fingers, they don't tire of the same, monotonous operations, are patient . . . and are highly productive. . . . This is why we prefer to use female workers in our plants" (Cowie, 2001, p. 119). Mexican women, Chinese women, and Navajo women were presented as "inherently and biologically flexible labor," with superdetailed capabilities (Nakamura, 2014, p. 929) for information technology labor.

From assemblage on the borderland to a product of Latina/o consumers, the radio, too, finds itself in this timeline. As consumers in the twentieth century, Latina/o listeners have used the analog Spanish radio stations as a mode of communication around immigrant rights and alerts on Immigration and Customs Enforcement (ICE) raids and as a mode of storytelling around immigration from Mexico and Latin America in the United States. Spanish radio in the United States has capitalized on the debates around immigration. ICE, too, has used Spanish radio as a technology of surveillance and intervention toward immigrant listeners (Casillas, 2014). But as Latina/os have increasingly used the internet, particularly through smartphones (Atske and Perrin, 2021), we see U.S. Citizenship and Immigration Services (USCIS) adapting this message online through websites such as that of the USCIS (Villa-Nicholas and Sweeney, 2019).

Building up to the digital age, the Mexican body in the United States was positioned as the mode by which new technologies were delivered back into Western markets, but the narrative of Latina/os as purely the blue-collar labor of the technology market is disrupted by Latina/o librarians and educators. In the 1970s, REFORMA, the national association to promote library and information services to Latina/os and

the Spanish speaking, was formed out of the Chicana/o and Latina/o
rights movements and momentum among Latina/o librarians. In 1971,
Arnulfo Trejo created REFORMA for Latina/o librarians to have an
amplified voice and to advocate for Spanish-speaking patrons' information needs. Latina/o librarians took an active approach to advocating for information technologies for their communities. Their
work resists the "library as neutral" trope we often see in the history
of libraries; rather, it demonstrates that Latina/o identity, or identity
politics, is directly entwined with and influences the ways in which
librarians approach programming with technology. Throughout their
careers, Latina/o librarians used information technologies to advocate
in parallel with Latina/o rights movements and often met with tension from the larger American Library Association. A look into the
information professions reveals that Latina/os were incorporating
their political and activist experiences outside of the library into their
work with technologies (Villa-Nicholas, 2015). Latina/o librarians
demonstrate that Latina/os have been developing ICTs such as software, databases, and websites and incorporating their identities into
the digital age since the 1960s (Villa-Nicholas, 2015).

The Twenty-First Century: The Digital Latina/o

As the internet increased in public use in the 1990s, information communication technologies jobs have served as intermediary roles for
immigrant Latina/os in various parts of their journey from Mexico
and Latin America into the United States. Schaeffer argues that Latina
women's bodies are commodities idealized by the Western gaze in the
neoliberal market as a mode of immigration through the internet. In
the neoliberal economy, the body, through cybermarriage, became "a
malleable and democratic surface that can be changed at will in the
search of becoming someone new" (Schaeffer, 2014, p. 124). For Latinas in the 1990s, cybermarriage to U.S. men became a moral, safe, and
middle-class avenue of immigration, in contrast with illegal border
crossing.

   With the emergence of public access to the internet, Mexican art-
ist Guillermo Gomez-Peña observed that enthusiasts of the "cyber
highway" were advocating that online identities brought postracial
color blindness. However, Gomez-Peña found the same tropes and

(Villa-Nicholas and Sweeney, 2019), and airports in heavily Latina/o areas throughout the United States began hosting anthropomorphized virtual agents (AVAs), coded as Latina, which worked as information support for travelers (Sweeney and Villa-Nicholas, 2022). These Latina AVAs are coded as *not undocumented*, embodying what Arlene Dávila (2001) calls the *Latino look*: light skin, straight hair, English-speaking first and Spanish-speaking second. They are sold by their manufacturers as efficient, with the ability to work without tiring and without the need to pass background checks. These Latina AVAs are built in the shadow of their Latina predecessors—Latina Information workers in telecommunications—but these AI's bypass the temporal inconvenience of Latina/os who are not assimilating quickly enough.

On Filipinos who work in call centers, Jan Padios has coined the concept of "Filipino/American relatability," which describes the relational demands of Filipino call center workers to "identify and communicate with U.S.-based Customers and therefore America as a material location and imaginary space" (Padios, 2018; Sweeney and Villa-Nicholas, 2022). Padios's research describes how affective notions of relatability become transformed into a social and cultural capital within the call center industry. We see this valued relatability bridged into Latina information work in telecommunications and built into Latina designed AVAs.

The borderland surveillance technology mediates "threatening" forms of Latinidad to remove that subject in the case of undocumented people, highly surveil Latina/o citizens that may be considered a "threat," or design acceptable forms of Latinidad through virtual agents. In telephony, the telephone has also been engaged to mediate Latinidad into an assimilated telephone operator and information worker. The technology engaged in telecommunications *buffered* the *Latino threat* that Chavez (2013) so vividly described. The telephone also demonstrates failures in U.S. cultural and linguistic pluralism—for example, the unwillingness to provide Spanish-speaking services to the public by phone companies even after court-ordered mandates to do so. For Spanish-speaking customers, this meant a lack of critical services to contact emergency services, their family members, and friends.

As Latina/os were recruited into telecommunications, telephony and the telephone were arranged to make sense of their identity and smooth out those features that were not Anglo and not Westernized enough. In sum, where we are at now in relation to the technological surveillance of the Latina/o data body is scaffolding off Latina/o technological labor for the past two centuries and is inseparable from the history of Latinas in telecommunications.

The Raced and Gendered Phone Company

From the inception of the Bell system, people of color and White women were discriminated against, laying the foundations for an unequal incorporation of Latinas into telecommunications. The state-oriented political economy came into conflict with that of the municipally oriented political economy, heavily shaping the Bell system. The history of the Bell system is an oscillating debate between private enterprise and public utilities (John, 2010). N. R. Danielian's canonical and definite history of Bell traces the imperial path of Bell's history of the telephone company. Danielian (1939) deems the early hierarchy as a "system of dictatorship" run by financial backers. Stephen Norwood (1990) has analyzed the gendered organization of work at Bell, as well as the activist response by White women operators. For an intersectional history of AT&T, Venus Green retells Bell's history as organized by race and gender; exclusions of people of color were done through the strained inclusion of White women as operators (Green, 2001). Drawing on their careful histories, this book extends their analysis to include the presence of workers of color in the industry, thus making visual their presence in labor history.

The following is a summary of those histories from the late nineteenth century to the 1960s, when the civil rights and affirmative action initiatives forced changes into AT&T. Four interrelated themes arise within this history: the decisions of the stockholders, administration, and managers to monopolize Bell; the general public, state, and federal attempts at taking custody of the telephone company; technological influences on labor, specifically the telephone operator; and the race, gendered, and class formations within AT&T. To contextualize this thesis, I parallel AT&T's history with that of Latinas in the United States, with a focus on labor, gender, and the Chicana/o rights movements.

The story of the Bell system begins with the invention of the telephone. The telephone then evolved in the United States through three different stages: commercialization, when the network was established

(1870s); popularization, when the network was developed into mass service (1900s); and naturalization, when the network was run by the federal government during World War I (1918–1919). Bell was first controlled by the owners of the majority of the stock during the early years of development, then by management with minority stock interest, and finally—in the early 1900s—by investment bankers (John, 2010; Danielian, 1939).

In 1876, Alexander Graham Bell obtained a basic patent for the "talking machine" and a second patent for the structural aspects of the telephone. Soon after, the Bell Patent Association was formed out of a group of investors funding Bell's work, leading to the inception of the Bell system. The zeal for science and invention of the nineteenth century complemented the patents for the telephone, obtained early on by Bell. This allowed for Bell to have the monopoly on telephone research and therefore propelled further invention.[2] Bell justified this monopoly with a narrative of "public good" through invention, a prelude that would contribute to technological progress in the United States today (Danielian, 1939).

From its early beginnings, the telephone was surrounded by controversy, debated between being a private good or a public utility that should be regulated by law (John, 2010). The United States privatizing the telephone is unique in that every other major developed country had deemed the telephone as a public good. Through this historical record, we see how the neoliberal ideology of privatizing public industries launched with Bell's decades-long fight with the U.S. government to maintain a private monopoly.

Advocates claimed that the telephone, telegraph, and postal system created "global villages," coining the phrase "Making a neighborhood of a Nation" around new systems of international communications (John, 2010, p. 10). However, like many technologies, the telephone was not created for the masses at its inception. The first users of the telephone were businessmen, professionals, merchants, and doctors; these users viewed the telephone as a tool that sped up the rate of production for those who could afford it. It was not until the late nineteenth century that the general public used telephones in commercial spaces such as markets. Because of boycotts and politicking spurred by high rates and a consequential demand for rate caps, this trend of public access to telephones ensued (John, 2010). Through the 1900s, public sentiment expressed that the telephone companies had an obligation to provide social services as well as to resist Bell's monopoly on the telephone (John, 2010; Green, 2001, p. 14). To assuage public fears, Bell president Theodore Vail used a new technique of business policy called "public relations."[3] In 1885, AT&T was established in New York in the name of "interconnection," an attempt at merging the telegraph and telephone service under one network as both a holding company and network provider (John, 2010, p. 209). Giving the U.S. public access to long-distance services and standardizing equipment presented the move toward "interconnection" as a public good (John, 2010; Danielian, 1939).[4] Also significant to this time period was the inception of the Pacific Bell Telephone Company in San Francisco in 1880, formed from the consolidation of the American Speaking Telephone Company and the National Bell Company. The expansion through the western states continued as Pacific Bell Telephone Company offered long-distance services in the late nineteenth century and incorporated smaller independent companies (Masters et al., 1927, p. 55).

Since the early twentieth century, the telephone operator has been a gendered job. Telephone operators started as young boys; however, their reputation for fighting with one another and rudeness toward the customers led to the intentional incorporation of White women.[5] The first woman telephone operator was hired in 1878 and was viewed with the "white collar" status of school teaching and clerking.[6] The first operators worked with different technical skills and challenges to connect callers, a short-lived process through the 1880s. Bell established a regimented and monotonous workplace for operators (Green, 2001; Norwood, 1990). The late nineteenth-century image of the operator shifted from a local worker who exchanged gossip with callers to a more controlled, "rationalized and scientifically managed workplace" (Green, 2001, p. 51). The shift in operators' duties was inspired by multiple factors, including managerial methods of control, more complex tasks such as more switchboard lines to monitor, and modifications to the switchboard technology in the name of efficiency, reliability, economy, and further control over the operator (John, 2010).[7] Bell modified technologies, such as the telephone operator cord board in order to further control or decrease labor altogether through "technological displacement" (Green, 2001).

Race, gender, and class are deeply embedded within Bell's formations of labor and technological changes. During the early years of the switchboard, a gendered "emotional labor" was intertwined with technological skills for the operator, as operators were trained to soothe. When equipment failure occurred, the operators were told to use their social skills to placate callers. In the nineteenth century, the utilization of the telephone in America was deeply gendered as well; from rural "farm wives" to urban wives, the telephone was used as a remedy for the isolation of gender roles (Brooks, 1976, p. 94).[8] But gender was not the only element in shaping the role of the telephone operator and use of the telephone in society. Race and class were key components in the status of the White woman telephone operator. The position of the operator was elite because it was exclusive to White women maintaining White status through the paternalistic ideologies of the Bell workplace. The model of passive "White woman" operator image maintained by the Bell system was also expected to be seen in places with poor working conditions and wages and other inadequate benefits. However, the early twentieth century would bring about labor resistance by White women telephone operators while simultaneously maintaining racial and class segregation within the workplace (Green, 2001; Brooks, 1976).

By the early twentieth century, the telephone had become popularized throughout the United States.[9] Despite their attempts, Bell was not the only operating company offering services. Because the Bell patent monopolies expired in the late nineteenth century, "independent" non-Bell companies built up their patent portfolios, operating 2.4 million telephones in 1902 compared to Bell's 3.1 million (John, 2010, p. 273). While Bell offered a larger network and a larger variety of calling plans, the independents offered lower rates for local services. But by 1907 the independent companies began to collapse, unable to compete with their Bell rival (John, 2010).

Although Bell continued to grow, public and lawmaker opinion still challenged the monopoly; the idea of government ownership over the phone company was a popular bipartisan idea in 1913 (John, 2010, p. 369). On the West Coast, the Bell Company expanded its ownership by acquiring smaller, already-established telephone companies. The name of the Pacific Bell Telephone Company changed to the Pacific Telephone and Telegraph Company in 1890, and then to the Pacific States Telephone and Telegraph Company in 1900 (Masters et al., 1927, p. 67). The Pacific States Telephone and Telegraph Company's name changed again to Pacific Telephone and Telegraph, acquiring the Sunset Telephone Company in 1906, which had recently merged with the Los Angeles Telephone Company.

In the early twentieth century, the use of telephone operators was not always popular among customers and phone companies. Independent companies had begun using the dial system, cutting out operators completely, but Bell defended the need for operators with a gendered campaign that advocated the "skill and faithfulness" of operators unavailable through machines (John, 2010, pp. 384–385).[10] At this time, the role of the operator continued to shift as well. The telephone-using public viewed the rural operator as an indispensable messaging center, presented as heroic for circulating news of emergencies around the country. Among Bell employees, operators began attending training schools, coached on how to talk and dress "simple." This persona maintained the white-collar distinction of the operator as a "lady" that separated the operators from factory assembly line workers, including the lower class, ethnic, racial, and language minorities (Norwood, 1990; Brooks, 1976).

Among the rank and file, working conditions were dissatisfying for telephone operators. Training manuals and technological changes to the switchboard limited the operator's skills, further standardizing working conditions. By the early twentieth century, labor unions increased all around, including the formation of the International Brotherhood of Electrical Workers (IBEW). Operators attempted to organize unions early on, however, male telephone union workers frequently foiled their efforts, unwilling to support women telephone workers in sympathy strikes.[11] In response to the exclusion of major unions such as the American Federation of Labor (AFL), local telephone operators formed nonaffiliated unions with international organizations (Green, 2001; Norwood, 1990).

Labor organizing and working conditions were executed not only by gender but also by racial exclusions. Although they held "white collar" jobs with a higher status symbol, White women telephone operators did so in poor working conditions and were expected not to challenge with strikes and organizing.[12] The telephone operators hired by Bell were done so based on their proficiency for speaking English and being of native-born British or Irish ancestry. Operator jobs were particularly discriminatory against minority groups deemed "foreigners, illiterate and untidy" (Norwood, 1990, p. 42), and Jews and Blacks were not allowed promotion beyond janitorial duties until 1940. The formation of the early telephone operator was used to appease the disgruntled male telephone customer. The racial exclusion of minorities was the foundation of Bell's employment and technological structure of control. White women telephone operators gained small social esteem through their work because it excluded racial minorities and was superior to factory conditions; however, the feminization of their occupation limited their real wage benefits (Green, 2001; Norwood, 1990).[13]

1918 was the only year that the Bell system was officially under government control, when President Woodrow Wilson issued an executive order transferring control of the telephone and telegraph to the Post Office Department under Postmaster General Burleson. The Bell system was officially a part of the U.S. Army communications, creating a Women's Telephone Operating Unit for those operators who were fluent in French and could interconnect lines with France.[14] Although Bell was officially under the post office, they would remain autonomous, assisting in using the telephone, telegraph, and cable as "one great medium" for the war. This time period worked out in Bell's benefit, giving them more leeway to explore wireless telegraphy, strengthen their logistical support, and create a network to allies. The unions also knew Postmaster General Burleson as an adversary, honoring fewer benefits than Bell and, consequentially, leading to more strikes by telephone employees (John, 2010).[15] Meanwhile on the West Coast, PT&T was experimenting with "telephotograph" equipment to transmit pictures as beams of light across the country. Also significant to the Pacific Coast's technological developments was direct radiotelephone communication with England, Scotland, and Wales (Masters et al., 1927). After the war, Bell entered the 1920s era with less regulation because of the failed attempt of government operations (Brooks, 1976).[16]

Unions and labor rights expanded from 1910 to 1930, providing more activist opportunities to the telephone operator. Telephone operators were taking on a new image as self-confident women, prepared to defend workers' rights. The newly formed Telephone Operator's Department within the International Brotherhood of Electrical Workers sent operators to worker union schools and organized conferences to bring unions together. In 1912 in Boston, operators formed one of the largest locals in the nation, the Women's Telephone Union

Local (WTUL) leading to victories in their demands of management and government in 1912 and 1919.[17] Despite the telephone operators' labor organizing of this time, which led to the formation of unions and successful strikes, Bell and male unions resisted. Despite union wins, the successful telephone workers' strikes were accomplished with men's terms in mind, neglecting female telephone operators (Norwood, 1990; Green, 2001, p. 108).[18]

But the technological changes of the 1920s, such as the increasing use of the dial system in Bell,[19] threatened unemployment for operators. The automated switching exchanges improved upon after World War I enabled Bell to treat operators as dispensable.[20] Manual operating boards were used for small cities and rural areas while automation was recommended for all but the largest cities. Dial and automation technologies led to a new role for operators, that of the "service specialist," operators known more as personal assistants in information. Technological shifts would also lead to more regimented working conditions. Although operators were overworked and underpaid, their labor in an exclusively White woman's occupation maintained their elite status as their jobs became closer to that of secretaries (Green, 2001).[21]

One result of the labor organizing from the 1920s was the development of the "family," an idea that would last through the 1970s and strongly resonate among employees of Bell/AT&T. Bell President Vail advanced the "family" concept as a way to curb involvement in unions via "employee associations," a concept used to displace trade unionism with nonunion benefits. About the "family," also known as the "Employees' Benefit Fund," Vail said, "We have felt more than ever that we are just one big family with every employee having a seat at the family table" (Green, 2001, p. 137). The employee associations were discussed by Bell management at conferences, where they planned to reinforce the gender expectations of White women operators via "sympathy," attempting to place White women in the familial role of passive and quiet, without a need for higher wages. Within the employee associations, representatives were elected to discuss wages and working conditions, however, without the power to actually change anything. The associations also placed operators on a "merit" based wage schedule, avoiding contractual union mandated raises. But being a member of the Bell family still held prestige for operators because of its racial homogeneity. Telephone operators' membership in this "family" reinstated racial hierarchies and accomplished Bell's larger goals of gaining higher profits via public relations (Green, 2001; Norwood, 1990), as I will explore in chapter 4.

The Depression and World War II changed labor and technology in the Bell system once again. Between 1929 and 1935, Bell cut their labor force by 40 percent; but these losses in employment were done to maintain the nine-dollar-per-share dividend (Danielian, 1939, p. 200). By 1930, Bell was providing more service to a record number of telephone customers and stockholders. However, in 1931, Bell experienced the first decline in telephone service, and by 1932, services were down by 10 percent (Brooks, 1976).

Although the economy recovered after the Depression, Bell did not replace operators' jobs, implementing the use of the dial instead. For those continuing operator work, workloads increased and working conditions declined. Green identifies this process of "technological displacement" as especially prevalent: it indicated Bell's intentional move to replace labor with automated systems (Green, 2001, p. 161). Despite the major cuts on Bell's part, by 1930, about two-thirds of the labor force were women (Danielian, 1939). Bell chose to squeeze more work out of telephone operators at an accelerated pace to make up for the losses, increasing the operators' average hourly load. Labor activism arose in response to the poor working conditions and low wages. In 1937, the U.S. Supreme Court upheld the Wagner Act, protecting independent labor organizing leading to the establishment of the National Federation of Telephone Workers (NFTW; Green, 2001, p. 173). Although women operators were still relegated to low representations among their male counterparts, they now engaged further in debates, bargaining demands, and work-related issues (Green, 2001; Danielian, 1939, p. 173).

The 1940s were rife with labor union wins for telephone workers, although not without setbacks. During the war, telephones became a crucial part of national communications. In 1942, long-distance calls increased by 400 percent immediately after Pearl Harbor (Brooks, 1976). Although World War II created a need for more telephone operators, it was used as an excuse for Bell managers to create new technologies as a method of "progress" to excuse the jobless rates. This was a key time for unnoticed technological displacement: "Low-paying operators' jobs could be sacrificed at the altar of 'progress'" (Green,

2001, p. 169). But despite technological displacement, the labor movement gained momentum in the mid-1940s with the first massive telephone worker walkouts, organized by the NFTW. The union won their
demands in 1946 for a ten-dollar-a-week increase and a minimum
hourly wage of sixty-five cents. In 1947, the NFTW created a new benefits package demand; however, when a deal could not be reached with
AT&T, more than three hundred thousand telephone workers walked
out, beginning the first nationwide strike in telephone history (Green,
2001; Brooks, 1976).

A significant shift ensued in gender and race roles for the operators
of the 1940s. White women telephone operators could not move into
other equivalent clerical jobs in the Bell system.[22] These new jobs were
not promotions but a horizontal transfer without wage increases or
training in skilled labor. African American employment also shifted
in the post-World War II jobs sector; under the Fair Employment
Practices Committee (FEPC), Blacks could now be hired into operator
roles (Green, 2001, p. 195). But this transition did not happen without
resistance from White operators, who degraded Black women through
minstrel shows in blackface. Bell used their own various discrimination tactics to ignore executive orders to integrate.[23] White operators
argued that Black women would threaten their social status and work
environments, and Bell used these complaints to justify their employment discrimination practices.[24] As the workplace was racially integrated, the image of the "White lady" telephone operator declined.
Bell restructured the workforce to diminish the "elite" operator status. As a result, telephone subscribers and White telephone operators
regularly harassed newly hired Black operators (Green, 2001).

Enter Latinas

Latinas entered telecommunications at a specific moment of social
change in the political, economic, racial, and gendered norms in the
United States. Latina/os had deep and contentious roots in the United
States long before the civil rights movements. During the Great
Depression from 1920 to World War II, over five hundred thousand
people of Mexican descent were either deported or repatriated (Blackwell, 2011, p. 44). Although Mexicans comprised less than 1 percent
of the U.S. population, they were targeted as 46 percent of all people

deported (Blackwell, 2011, p. 44). Due to a labor shortage during World War II, migrant workers were brought back into the United States to work on agricultural production. After the postwar boom, the U.S. program "Operation Wetback" targeted Mexicans through massive deportation. Under the "Bracero Program" from 1942 to 1964, Latina/os were excluded from labor unions and paid low wages for seasonal work, viewed as disposable by agricultural employers. In fact, Latina/os were segregated from labor unions and often subject to hostility by the AFL when they received membership, separated into lower pay rates and seniority lines.[25] With increased suppression came increased activism among Latina/os in California, who organized labor strikes in Oxnard, California, in 1903 and a massive movement among cannery workers in the 1940s (Blackwell, 2011).

The Bell system continued their lip service toward recruiting previously excluded minorities throughout the 1960s, however, without greatly diversifying the workplace. AT&T developed the "Plan for Progress," a voluntary set of affirmative action agreements that were not mandatory. Although women and men of color employees increased during these years, the computerization and occupational segregation also decreased the number of jobs in these sectors. Bell also developed expanded direct distance dialing (DDD), allowing subscribers to dial their calls long distance with minimum operator assistance, further diminishing their need for operators (Green, 2001).

For the telephone operator, the decline of the "White lady" image and integration of Black women were used as methods of control in the workplace, manipulating White workers through threatening their jobs by hiring racial minorities. Bell management also decreased the privileges previously afforded to White operators, such as free coffee, tea, and comfortable lunchrooms. Telephone workers of color lacked union representation, as union officials saw themselves only acting on behalf of White workers' interests, viewing new minority hiring as a threat to White union members' jobs. The 1960s were a time when racial tensions and resistance to workplace integration mounted, leading to the pivotal turning point of the *EEOC v. AT&T* case of the 1970s (Green, 2001).

Civil rights movements of the 1960s drew negative attention to the Bell system. Reports of discrimination and low numbers of the recruitment of people of color and White women placed Bell in the spotlight of workplace integration. In 1975, the U.S. government conducted its second antitrust investigation into AT&T, which would lead to the breakup of the Bell system in 1984. Civil unrest, the Bell monopoly, the civil rights movements, and the feminist movements built up to 1970, when the Federal Communications Commission denied AT&T's request for raising interest rates, inciting the official investigation into discriminatory employment hiring practices (Brooks, 1976; Green, 2001).

The social unrest of the 1960s led to increased affirmative action legislation to integrate the workplace. Throughout the 1950s and 1960s, Latina/os were largely excluded from blue-collar jobs and union membership. By the 1970s, Latina/os were more widely incorporated into the workplace, however, in conjunction with the recession from 1974 to 1975, the economy was becoming deindustrialized, two trends leading to fewer jobs for newly incorporated minorities. These new market trends were the beginnings of the political economy we now know as "neoliberalism," with trends in corporate restructuring to diminish union rights and the backing of the government to defund public services. The brief window of affirmative action integration that Latinas would benefit from had closed quickly after the 1970s, with the implementation of the Reagan era, a time when many cities would lose industrial employment (Segura and Zavella, 2007).

Despite the affirmative action implementation, the standard of living for Latina/os dropped from 1973 to 1987. Poverty rates rose three times higher for Latina/os than their Anglo counterparts. While there was a 70 percent rise of Latinas in the workforce, Latina workers in the United States occupied the lowest ranks of the wage labor force by the mid-1970s. In 1970, 18 percent of Latina hourly workers earned poverty-level wages, and those Latinas in blue-collar jobs often saw their job sent overseas to workers exploited for even lower wages. For Latina/os who retained their jobs, they continued to experience decreased wages and benefits. Between 1975 and 1989, average earnings growth among Latina/os slowed to the point of stagnation as income inequality grew (Vélez-Ibáñez and Sampaio, 2002, p. 54).

Latinas entered telecommunications just as the economy was further liberalizing, unions were losing more than gaining in the labor sector, and technology was rapidly accelerating.

2

THE INVISIBLE
INFORMATION WORKER

In 1973, the consent decree between the Equal Employment Opportunity Commission and the American Telephone and Telegraph Company led to the employment of Latinas, White women, and blue-collar information workers. But the *EEOC v. AT&T* case suggests a historical precedent of Latina exclusion in STEM, IT, internet, and telecommunications-related fields. The *EEOC v. AT&T* consent decree, an equal employment affirmative action mandate for underrepresented people, settled decades-long filings of employment discrimination toward White women and women and men of color. Latinas entered the lower levels of the telecommunications field with the consent decree settlement, beginning lifelong careers under the Bell system[1] as telephone operators, customer service representatives, data entry operators, and electrical engineers, to name just a few. Latinas had long been overlooked in telecommunications and IT fields more broadly, as demonstrated by the EEOC report *A Unique Competence*, the case proceedings, and the consent decree.

As a result of the *EEOC v. AT&T* case, Latinas entered the lower levels of the Bell system as invisible information laborers. The *EEOC v. AT&T* case contributed to the underdevelopment of Latinas in management and highly skilled positions of STEM, IT, and telecommunications. A focus on the *EEOC v. AT&T* case with an eye toward Latinas (1) contextualizes the environment in which Latinas entered technological fields; (2) suggests the importance of intersectional race, gender, and class considerations of affirmative action movements; and (3) uncovers the invisible Latina labor in telecommunications and

43

internet support. Because of the stagnation of Latinas as white- and blue-collar low-wage workers in information technology fields, we do not see the effect of *Latinidad* on IT and internet companies in visible ways.

In this chapter, I seek to explore the historical circumstances surrounding Latinas' information labor employment during the monumental impact of affirmative action on telecommunications. I look at how the National Organization for Women (NOW) and the EEOC erased color with the EEOC report *A Unique Competence*. Next, I question the effectiveness of the case proceedings for Latinas with regard to evidence. Finally, I examine the consent decree and its results to gain an understanding of the discourse excluding Latina information workers. This chapter searches for Latinas within the historic EEOC v. AT&T case, outlining how Latinas were further eclipsed in telecommunications and acknowledging the historical moment that Latinas became information laborers.

Latinas Enter Tech Fields

Although a current recognition of the underrepresentation of Latinas in larger tech corporations has come to the public's attention (Feliú-Mójer, 2014), the process of exclusion and inclusion (through affirmative action) of Latinas into related private sectors reaches back to civil rights–era protests and legislation (Acuña and Compeán, 2008). The 1970s saw a significant entrance for Latinas into telecommunications after such monumental cases as the Civil Rights Act of 1965, the Voting Rights Act, and the creation of the EEOC under Title VII, "which prohibits employment discrimination on the basis of race, color, religion, national origin, and sex" (Green, 2012). Once omitted from employment in jobs, such as the telephone operator and clerk positions, Latinas were suddenly eligible for AT&T positions after the mandate of the consent decree. Considering the racial and gendered contexts of telecommunication policy acknowledges that Latinas were in technological spaces built on Whiteness (de la Peña, 2010) and supplanted by gender-only discourse. Including intersectional backgrounds of Latinas in the United States shifts the history of telecommunications and technology into multidimensional accounts.

Because of the shifting racial constructions in the United States, Latinas' entrance into the telecommunications sector has not fit easily into the racial binary framed by the EEOC-AT&T consent decree.[2] Due to the "gender first" priorities of NOW and the EEOC's legal approach, Latinas were especially neglected (Green, 2012, p. 45). Main players involved in the consent decree made Latinas' entrance into telecommunications peripheral. As a result, Latinas entered the lower levels of the field of the Bell system as an invisible minority. The *EEOC v. AT&T* case contributed to the groundwork of a field presently underrepresented by Latinas working with sophisticated technological skills and oversaturated with Latinas in blue-collar information worker positions. The disregard for women of color's intersectional needs set a precedent of inadequate "inclusions" into technological spaces.

Although a solid foundation of scholarship exists around the history of the *EEOC v. AT&T* consent decree, a deficit of analysis around Latina presence weakens the body of literature on telecommunications. Venus Green (2012) conducted the most thorough investigations into the ways in which the EEOC, influenced by NOW, separated gender and race, with White women benefiting the most. Green named this "gender-first" approach as a large cause as to why Black working-class women's complaints were neglected in the post–consent decree years at AT&T. NOW minimized the differences among women's testimonies, thereby erasing Blackness from complaints filed by African American women against AT&T, instead taking the approach of universalizing women. Marjorie Stockford's (2004) historical account argues that the EEOC focused solely on race, neglecting gender altogether. Despite the EEOC leading the suit against AT&T, tensions were high between NOW and the EEOC. Women from NOW, as well as women staff at the EEOC, found the EEOC dismissive of issues around gender; Stockford recalls, "For the EEOC's part, NOW, a feminist organization only three years old, was hardly in its lawyers' consciousness. Theoretically the two groups were working toward the same goal, but they had little respect for each other" (Stockford, 2004, p. 23). Stockford (2004) recollects White feminist influence on EEOC attorneys as a necessary step in awareness. However, feminist organizations such as NOW turned a blind eye to race as a result of lobbying the EEOC. But Stockford universalized "women," presented as receiving the same discriminations across the board when convenient for the argument.[3] Louis Katheryn Herr (2003) gives a similar gender-centric retelling of the history leading up to the consent decree, with particular emphasis on NOW's role in pressuring AT&T through protests and organizing female employees.

The class divides within the affirmative action movements also worked against women of color, whose working-class needs were different than those of middle-class feminists, as seen in the employment discrimination case *EEOC v. Sears, Roebuck, & Co.*, a 1973 investigation that went to trial in 1985. Class ideologies within feminism benefited middle-class feminists, neglected lower-class feminists, and impacted the lawsuit (Zuckerman, 2008).

MIT professor and former EEOC researcher Phyllis Wallace examined the results of the case from various disciplines, including industry, psychology, economics, sociology, business, and management. Researchers looked at employment disparities among White men, White women, Black women, and Black men. Employment discrimination within the Bell system was by occupation and not by wage within occupation (Wallace and Nelson, 1976, p. 3). Due to the limited information available, research on Latinas is thin in Wallace's collected essays.

Latinas now lag drastically in representation in STEM fields, IT workplaces, and telecommunications (Jaschik, 2014). This history struggles with race not only as an epistemology[4] but also as a fluid scale, upon which Latinas are positioned depending on the historical, social, gendered, and political moment. The *EEOC v. AT&T* case, framed by a racial Black and White binary and reorganized with "gender-first" arguments that neglected race, demonstrates the undertones of impossibility for Latinas entering into technological spaces. Within the *EEOC v. AT&T* case, Latinas identified as one- or two-dimensional subjects, by national origin or as Spanish-speaking minorities, and had no entrance into the *EEOC v. AT&T* moment.

RACE CLASSIFICATIONS

In the recently formed western United States, racial constructs around Latina identity were fluid and unstable. The question as to whether

Mexicans considered themselves White was contested within and outside of the community. Although labeled White since the Treaty of Guadalupe Hidalgo in 1848, Mexicans were often treated as second-class citizens by Anglo society, not fitting easily into the Black-White racial binary that structures the United States (MacLean, 2006). Despite some privilege Mexican Americans gained as being White-identified, they lacked higher education institutions of any kind and had no national civil rights organizations. Though historically important for minorities in the United States, the Voting Rights Act (VRA) of 1965 did not directly affect Latina/os until 1975, when it expanded to language minorities (Garcia, 1997). Despite evidence that favored separating Spanish-surnamed people as a group, historical records, such as the census, grouped Latina/os as "other minorities" with American Indians and Asians. Title VII of the Civil Rights Act provided Latina/os the opportunity to identify as people of color, recognizing their differences from Anglos and ethnic White European immigrants.

In the 1960s, Latina/os were not surveyed as a separate racial group, so the possibility of comparing numbers of Latinas in telecommunications is difficult. Besides working as migrant farmworkers, Latina/os were heavily involved in the steelworkers' sector, the automobile industry, the smelter workers' sector, and the rubber industry (Acuña and Compeán, 2008, p. 345). Despite laborers winning more labor rights in the previous decade, the post–World War II era saw disinvestment in the unionized industries where Latina/os had just arrived, their new workplaces being reshaped by the neoliberal era.[5] These changes resulted in shifting jobs away from manufacturing and into the service sector, increasing high technology industry jobs, and the sending of jobs overseas (Gómez-Quiñones, 1994, p. 332). In the 1960s, Latinas worked overwhelmingly in operatives, service work, food processing, and electronics, as well as in telecommunications and the garment industry. In 1960, 8.6 percent of Latinas worked in professional occupations, such as teaching, nursing, librarianship, and social work; however, most Latinas worked in the "secondary" sector of the labor market, which included jobs in sales, clerical, operatives, and non-farm labor, household work, low-level (other) service work, and farm labor. In 1970, Latinas made up 33.9 percent of the secondary sector occupations, compared to 43.4 percent White women, 21.4 percent African American women, and 30.2 percent Native American women

(Hesse-Biber and Carter, 2005, pp. 54–57). For Latinas, the *EEOC v. AT&T* time period marked shifts in identity markers such as race, gender, labor, and political identities.[6]

A Unique Competence

A number of reports demonstrated the lack of Latina/o employees in the phone company. In 1966 at Pacific Telephone, only 7 percent of directory assistance operators were Spanish-surnamed. Out of 348 subjects in 1969, Southern Bell employed no Spanish-surnamed toll operators, with 70 percent White women and 23 percent Black women making up the ethnic grouping. From 1970 to 1971, 11 percent of toll, directory assistance, and traffic service staffers at twelve different locations were Spanish surnamed compared to 43 percent White women and 46 percent Black women. In clerical occupations from 1970 to 1971 at twelve different locations in the Bell system, 20 percent of Spanish-surnamed employees held positions compared to 40 percent White and 40 percent Blacks. In Felix M. Lopez's Bell system report (1976), Spanish-surnamed workers were significantly lower in numbers among telephone operators. In spite of the drastic evidence of exclusion, the EEOC report filed against AT&T, *A Unique Competence*, did not explore Latinas beyond linguistic and national-origin discriminations. Latinas were presented as one-dimensional victims, excluding the nuances of race and gender.

From the beginning, the EEOC and collaborating ethnic organizations fell short in including Latinas in the *EEOC v. AT&T* preliminary proceedings. The case that became *EEOC v. AT&T* began in 1970 when the Federal Communications Commission blocked AT&T's attempt at raising long-distance rates until the company agreed to stop employment discrimination practices. The EEOC conducted an investigation into the ways in which AT&T's discrimination was executed. They found that the systematic discrimination by race, sex, and national origin affected advertising, hiring, training, promotions, pay, benefits, career promotion, and vacation leave. The report also analyzed the gendered classifications at work: "Every single wage-earning job was classified as male or female. . . . 'The Bell monolith,' the government study found, 'is, without doubt, the largest oppressor of women workers in the United States'" (MacLean, 2006, p. 132). As a constituency,

Latina/os accounted for nearly all the complaints filed with the EEOC labeled as "national origin." An especially significant method of discrimination, which AT&T defended as good business, was the "word-of-mouth" approach to recruiting. This tactic inevitably led to excluding minorities, especially Spanish-speaking people.

On December 1, 1971, the EEOC filed *A Unique Competence: A Study of Equal Employment Opportunity in the Bell system*, a large manuscript detailing AT&T discrimination with footnotes, charts, tables, and testimonies (Herr, 2003, p. 63). According to the report, "Spanish-surnamed Americans"[7] were excluded from employment in numerous ways. The EEOC named Spanish-surnamed Americans as the "Invisible Minority" in the Bell system (Herr, 2003, p. 67), finding that Spanish-surnamed Americans were specifically excluded from Bell employment. While the primary focus was sex discrimination, the EEOC acknowledged Black women and Latinas as the most neglected or outright discriminated against. Out of the twelve Standard Metro-politan Statistical Areas (SMSAs) where the Latina/o population was the largest, Bell's employment rates were nowhere close to the industry average: "In none of the twelve SMSA's which had a substantial His-panic population was their employment by the operating companies at rates near their representation in the workforce" (Wallace and Nel-son, 1976, p. 259). The reason for the underrepresentation of Latina/os was because the preemployment criteria, including paper credentials and test scores, "tended to screen out a disproportionate number of minorities" (Wallace and Nelson, 1976, p. 259). The major complaints filed in *A Unique Competence* solely focus on Latina/os as language minorities of "Spanish ancestry," engaging the Bell system discrimina-tions against Latina/os without racial or gendered components.

A Unique Competence addressed the employment discrimination toward Latina/o customers and employees in the final chapter of the report. Although concluding the report with "The Invisible Minor-ity," the EEOC disregarded the nuances of the "Spanish-surnamed" group. The EEOC came to five conclusions about Spanish-surnamed employees by Bell: they were employed at a rate significantly lower than their proportion to the population; Spanish-surnamed employ-ees at Bell were working in the lowest-paid classifications and excluded from all management; Spanish-surnamed employees positions in Bell were equal to Blacks in Southern companies in the previous decade; Bell's recruitment and hiring policies, aimed at restricting/ excluding Black employment, had a greater impact on Spanish-surnamed employees; and finally, Bell had made no efforts to improve the employment states of Spanish-surnamed employees. They were estimated to have lost more than $137 million annually due to their positions in the lowest-paying jobs or outright denial of employment altogether (Papers of Marjorie Stockford, 1971, p. 288). Of the twelve SMSAs identified in the report, Spanish-surnamed employees did not rise above 1 percent of employees at AT&T, and those few employed made 78 percent of the earnings of their White counterparts. *A Unique Competence* discussed the lack of services as particularly problematic. The investigation found that Bell had only one Spanish-surnamed interviewer and that the interview process itself held cultural biases, allowing for many reasons to disqualify a Latina/o candidate from hiring (Papers of Marjorie Stockford, 1972, p. 1276). The Bell companies, with the exception of New Jersey Bell, hired installers with fluent English proficiency who could pass the Wonderlic Test in English and could meet the height standards for the average Anglo.⁵ *A Unique Competence* found that all these demands worked against the recruitment of Latina/o employees to the Bell system. Although *A Unique Competence* ends with AT&T's astounding tactics of discrimination, the report grouped Latina/os into a monolithic contingent of the "Spanish-surnamed," neglecting to investigate intersectional biases of race and gender unique to Latinas.

Testimonies and Evidence

Despite the weighty evidence, proceedings continued to treat Latinas as solely language and national origin minorities, neglecting racial and gendered components. These complaints were filed through ethnic organizations born out of the civil rights movements, working on the state and national level in various sectors of U.S. politics, education, and employment. Ethnic organizations and NOW brought political pressure on the EEOC during the 1960s and 1970s to enforce Title VII of the Civil Rights Act, leading to major cases such as *EEOC v. AT&T*. Though the EEOC was created to enforce Title VII, it did not gain the political momentum it needed until the early 1970s when it targeted AT&T as the largest private-sector employer and the largest overall employer of women. AT&T's discriminations against Latina/os were racially motivated; however, because the case was built on a framework with race discussed as "White and Black" and that was gender-universalized to benefit White women, Latinas had little more ground than language and national origin complaints.

Prior to the *EEOC v. AT&T* case, Latina/os, and Mexicans in particular, had a tense relationship with the EEOC. In a regional EEOC conference in San Francisco in 1966, executive director Hermen Edelsberg told a Mexican American audience that the EEOC did nothing about Mexican American problems because "Mexican Americans were 'distrustful of agencies,' so little could be done. He even told his listeners that Mexicans had 'no such proverb as "the wheel that squeaks the loudest gets the grease"'" (MacLean, 2006, p. 169). A few weeks later at an Albuquerque conference, fifty Mexican American leaders gathered to meet with the EEOC chairperson Franklin Delano Roosevelt Jr., but Roosevelt sent Edelsberg instead. The leaders met until 3:00 a.m., walking out on the EEOC the next day as a united body (MacLean, 2006, p. 170). This walkout simultaneously demonstrated a rejection of the state of the EEOC as well as the unity of a Mexican American constituency, which became the Mexican American Ad Hoc Committee on Equal Employment.

The Mexican American Legal Defense and Education Fund was one of the organizing entities crucial to Latina/o engagement in this case. Founded in 1967 in Los Angeles, California (Vigil, 2000, p. 238), MALDEF used several strategies to gain rights for Latina/os, including litigation, advocacy, educational outreach, law school scholarships, immigration policy, and leadership development (p. 239). But MALDEF and other ethnic organizations were unprepared to incorporate gender into their proceedings.[9] MALDEF's involvement in the EEOC case advocated for further recruitment of Latina/o employees in higher-paying jobs at the Bell system and better services for Spanish-speaking customers and challenged the exploitation of current Latina/o employees. The nature of the witness testimonies in MALDEF records neglected Latinas, primarily focusing on bilingual services, problems with employment services, the Bell system's participation in the Spanish-speaking community, regional attitudes of Mexican Americans toward the Bell system, effects of media and communication on the Chicano image, community organizations' experiences with Bell, customer experience within the Spanish-speaking community, education among the Spanish-speaking community, bilingual services, and Bell employment (Alvarado, MALDEF records, 1972). None of the testimonies focused specifically on Latina needs, employment experiences, customer experiences, or the overall impact of Latinas in particular.

From April 17 to April 21, 1972, MALDEF and the California Rural Legal Assistance held testimonies of witnesses in the case, concerned with the Pacific Telephone and Telegraph Company's treatment of Latina/os and Asian Americans.[10] Testimonies were also taken from representatives of Spanish-speaking communities from May 8 to 12 in New York (Wallace and Nelson, 1976, p. 249). The testimonies came from Latina/o customers and employees of the Bell system: "All these potential speakers shared one goal: to document orally why the phone company should itself suffer in exchange for the suffering it had caused its own employees" (Stockford, 2004, p. 114).

Due to the lack of Latina AT&T employees, Latina customer testimonies were the dominant witnesses on record. However, they do indicate markers of racial and gendered experiences. Dolores Martinez of Healdsburg, California, testified that she was involved in an accident. Unable to reach help on the telephone, Martinez walked three miles for emergency help (MALDEF records, 1972b). Maria Torres, also from Healdsburg, had a child with heart problems whose doctor was located in San Francisco. On days when she expected calls from the doctor, Torres had to keep her children home due to the lack of bilingual phone services. Domitila Reyes of Windsor, California, had a number of negative incidents with the phone company. Reyes received a series of erroneous bills from the phone company that had been previously paid. She was unable to call the police during an auto accident and unable to get her son out of jail in San Diego because of a lack of telephone services in Spanish (MALDEF records, 1972b). The witness list also contained one testimony from Maria Marquez, a rejected applicant of AT&T. Although sparse, the types of issues testified on AT&T services demonstrated the intersectional gender roles of Latinas.

The FCC hearing's evidence was further presented as solely linguistic, neglecting race and gender. During the FCC hearings, CRLA lawyer Albert Moreno proposed the FCC place a call in Spanish to

Sonoma County. The caller claimed to have an emergency in order to see the results of service to Spanish speakers. Guido del Prado, a Spanish-speaking client of Moreno's, called information in Sonoma County. The transaction was passed to two different telephone operators, totaling six minutes and forty seconds of wait time before del Prado got the information he needed (Stockford, 2004, p. 119). This session ignored the real-life circumstances described above by Latinas, overlooking gendered and racially organized situations experienced by Latinas unable to use the telephone.

The Attitudinal Survey of Latina/o experiences of Pacific Telephone & Telegraph revealed great dissonance with the phone company, demonstrating racially motivated biases experienced by Latina/os. Prepared by Manuel Alvarado, former director of community education for South Alameda County, this survey detailed the results of a door-to-door survey conducted in the county among Mexican Americans "to determine their attitudes, impressions, and experiences in regard to Pacific Telephone & Telegraph service and employment" (Alvarado, 1972). Eighty-six random respondents were surveyed on Bell services to Mexican Americans and Spanish speakers. Respondents of the survey overwhelmingly required Spanish-speaking telephone operators, indicating that Anglos were more likely to receive better PT&T services and jobs. Respondents acknowledged that the telephone company discriminated against Mexican Americans in services and jobs, finding it difficult to make telephone calls and pay telephone bills because of the English-only services. Despite the employment discrimination, seventy-nine respondents would apply for installer, operator, and management jobs if the telephone company really advertised to hire Mexican Americans. Finally, eighty-one out of eighty-three respondents favored a Mexican American–owned and operated company in Alameda County because it would offer Spanish-speaking services. The survey reveals a racial consciousness in Latina/o respondents' experience as potential employees and customers (Alvarado, 1972).

The resulting PT&T objectives, though lofty in promises of employment and improved services, continued to deny the intersectional needs of Latinas. In a press release in March 1972, PT&T announced major goals to include Spanish-speaking and/or Mexican American employees and customers. PT&T's promises included doubling the

number of "Spanish-Americans" in its employment by 1975 and tri-
pling the number of "Spanish-Americans" by 1980 (MALDEF records,
1972c). PT&T also guaranteed that 25 percent of all new hires would
be "Spanish-American" employees, including 30 percent of all new
college management hires. PT&T guaranteed to take responsibility
for hiring one thousand Spanish-speaking-only persons. The "Press
Summary of Bell Telephone Hearings on Spanish-Speaking Employment Problems" omitted Latina employment recruitment, services, or
training at PT&T (MALDEF records, 1972c).

The Impact of the Consent Decree for Latinas

White women and women of color in particular were discriminated
against in a number of ways at the Bell companies. However, Latinas
were made invisible because of the emphasis put on race by federal
laws and political organizing group politics (Green, 2001, p. 61). Not-
withstanding numerical evidence, NOW and the EEOC's arguments
lost the nuanced experiences of women of color by becoming gender focused (Stockford, 2004). NOW identified race discrimination
as a problem within the Bell system but did not use African American
women's testimonies as charges for sex discrimination, labeling their
statements as racially motivated discriminations (Green, 2001, p. 53).
Thus the consent decree fell short, dichotomizing Latinas' identity as
only significant with respect to language services.

On January 18, 1973, the consent decree was handed down before
the U.S. District Court for the Eastern District of Pennsylvania (Wallace and Nelson, 1976, p. 252). The consent decree put into place col-
lective bargaining rights, a pay-promotion plan, and more promotion
opportunities for "females and minorities"; changed standardized testing so that scores could not discriminate against potential employees;
ensured that female college graduates were hired directly into management; and guaranteed pay adjustments and back pay for previous
discrimination. Reports, surveys, and testimonies from Latina/o communities went unacknowledged, lumping Latinas into the "women or
minorities" category essential to the consent decree. Latinas continued to be made invisible through the end of the *EEOC v. AT&T* case.
The direct impact of the consent decree on Latinas is difficult to index
due to the discrepancies in censuses. Although no longer categorized

as "White" on surveys, Latinas were still reported as "other" with all minorities except African Americans. Herbert R. Northrup and John A. Larson's (1979) *The Impact of the AT&T-EEO Consent Decree* noted, "Minority group members achieved the greatest gains in regions where they represent a relatively significant proportion of the population" (p. 98). According to Northrup and Larson, males and females of the same racial group tended to do well in the same job category, and different racial groups had success in different sectors of AT&T (See table 2.1). Although there was a shortage of technically trained Black workers, their numbers far exceeded the available amount of Latina/os and other minorities, particularly American Indians. Latina/os suffered the additional barriers of language and cultural differences, thereby compounding the problem of assimilating them into the AT&T labor force (Northrup and Larson, 1979, p. 98).

Data on Latinas presence in AT&T by regions demonstrate a slow and steady incline in the percentage of Latina employees in the Mountain and Pacific region (Northrup and Larson, 1979). Table 2.1 demonstrates the small increase of Latina employees in the Mountain region, within a 1 to 2 percent range in both the white- and blue-collar jobs. In the Pacific region, the greatest significant increase in employment was for Latinas in blue-collar jobs. Over the six years surveyed, the increase of Latina information worker jobs was minor. Despite the

TABLE 2.1
REGIONAL INCREASE OF LATINA EMPLOYEES AT AT&T
AFTER THE CONSENT DECREE

Year/region	Latina employees at AT&T (%)	Total Latina/o employees at AT&T (%)
1973, Mountain Region	White collar: 12.1 Blue collar: 10.6	White collar: 9.9 Blue collar: 10.8
1979, Mountain Region	White collar: 13.3 Blue collar: 12.0	White collar: 11.6 Blue collar: 10.1
1973, Pacific Region	White collar: 8.2 Blue collar: 6.8	White collar: 7.3 Blue collar: 8.0
1979, Pacific Region	White collar: 9.9 Blue collar: 10.1	White collar: 9.2 Blue collar: 9.7

Source: Northrup and Larson, 1979, pp. 172–185.

circumstantial oversight of intersectional needs for Latina employees, Latinas did become information laborers in the Bell system. Many Latinas began employment as telephone operators, and as their work became automatic, they transferred into such jobs as data entry personnel, customer service agents, clerks, and technicians (Villa-Nicholas, 2014). Latina information workers provided the backbone and hidden information labor that contributed to popular access to the internet, building infrastructure such as cable-wireless networks and providing customer support that underwrote the creation, evolution, and access of the supporting hardware and software of the internet.

Independent Companies

The history of independent companies and the divestiture of AT&T in the long run matters to Latina telephone operators because they experienced firsthand the constant shifting identities of these companies. Bell "diversified" in the early 1970s, and the consent decree went on to impact many other phone companies that were broken off from Bell.

The landmark case against AT&T deeply impacted competing phone companies as well. Independent phone companies had sparred for decades to break up the monopoly of AT&T, and the EEOC-AT&T consent decree had a rippling impact on those companies that were still in business. In the nineteenth century, as Bell's patents expired, independent telephone companies began competing more intensely and opening their business in Midwest and Southern towns and in the rural and farming areas that were often overlooked by Bell. But it was through hindering independent companies' growth through acquisitions and not allowing those companies to connect to their long-distance telephone lines that AT&T was ultimately able to become a true monopoly that ran the telephone lines in the United States by 1910 (Green, 2001, p. 14), and Bell became the primary shareholder of their biggest competitor, Western Union. Bell continued to grow by monopolizing patents over their advancements in telephone technology, often done by undermining or even stealing the inventions of their competitors (Wu, 2011; Wilson and Teske, 1990). With that growth came the purchase of independent phone companies throughout the twentieth century. By 1934, AT&T controlled 80 percent of U.S. telephones and long-distance calls (Wilson and Teske, 1990), rendering independent companies often vulnerable to the power of the AT&T monopoly.

Divestiture—1980s

In 1982, AT&T signed a consent decree for divestiture, planning to split up the monolith into small Bell Operating Companies (BOCs). The breakup of Bell through divestiture led to seven regional companies: NYNEX, acquired by Bell Atlantic in 1996, which became Verizon and is now Frontier; Pacific Telesis, acquired by SBC in 1997, now AT&T; Ameritech, acquired by SBC in 1999, now AT&T; Bell Atlantic, acquired by SBC in 1999, now AT&T; Southwestern Bell Corporation, turned into SBC, now AT&T; and U.S. West, acquired by Qwest in 2000, turned into CenturyLink in 2011 (Tunstall, 1985).

Throughout AT&T's growth and life span, there was a push-pull between the company, the government, and independent telecommunications companies to resist monopoly growth and attempt to regulate the monolith. By 1970, when Latinas were intentionally recruited into telephone companies, most independents had been incorporated into AT&T.

General Telephone and Electronics Corporation (GTE) was one such company. GTE was a telephone company and electronics manufacturer in the United States from 1952 to 1982 (Encyclopedia Britannica, n.d.). In 1958, GTE had a moment in its history where it posed a threat to the monolith that was AT&T, when GTE merged with Sylvania Electronics, which positioned them as a potential rival to AT&T because of their capability to "manufacture the electronic switching systems needed by a phone company" (Encyclopedia Britannica, n.d.). GTE primarily serviced rural areas where AT&T was unavailable. GTE also served California suburbs and Tampa, Florida. Its California service areas became a central recruiting area for Latina telephone operators. GTE also conducted data processing in 1979 with their purchase of Telenet. Ultimately, GTE merged with Bell Atlantic Corporation and became Verizon Communications in 2000. As Latinas worked as landline operators and in customer service, they found themselves transitioning into Verizon, and by 2015, Frontier Communications Corporation purchased all the Verizon landlines across the country.

A Latina/o Centered Phone Company

Throughout the 1970s, litigation against the Bell system increased among the Latina/o community, especially regarding the lack of Spanish-speaking telephone services. As a follow-up to the 1973 consent decree, Latina/o rights groups such as MALDEF found that AT&T was "noncompliant with the 1973 consent decree" in that they neglected to promote Latina/o workers, denied new hire positions to Latina/o workers, and failed to recruit minorities (labeled as Chicanos) to apply for new hire positions (Hamilton, 1975, p. 1). Latina/o rights groups went on to conduct detailed surveys of the Spanish-speaking populations, particularly in northern California, who were customers of PT&T.

The Spanish Language Assistance Bureau (SLAB) was the Spanish-speaking telephone operator service that PT&T contracted. However, ongoing lawsuits from Latina/o rights groups, such as Los Padrinos (*the godfathers*), found that there were gaps in PT&T's procedures, and English-speaking telephone operators had no process to transfer calls to SLAB. Los Padrinos interrogated PT&T throughout the 1970s as a follow-up to the consent decree in order to close the gap time in telephone operator response for calls in Spanish, especially for emergency service calls (Evangelista and Gonzales, 1975). The women that I interviewed conducted all their operator services in English and engaged in Spanish at home. They described Spanish-speaking operating services as a separate office where all language services were conducted.

Indeed, the Spanish language section was not only separated from the English-speaking telephone operators; it was compartmentalized so that it was *only* spoken at the cord board or answering service. So severe was the segregation of Spanish-speaking telephone operators and the rules that restricted them that in 2000, Premier Operating Services—a contractor for operating services—was sued by the EEOC and thirteen bilingual Mexican and Mexican American telephone operators. In this case, Premier had an "English-only" policy that prohibited employees from speaking Spanish *except* for with customers. Mexican and Mexican American telephone operators were prohibited from speaking Spanish anywhere else on the company premises: "The policy was posted at the entrance to the building where Premier was located, along with a notice that 'conspicuously couple[d] the policy with a warning about weapons, implying a combined concern about the conduct of those persons who speak a language other than English'" (Colón, 2002). Those Latina/o workers had to sign a memo agreeing to only speak Spanish with customers or outside of the building. Six of those employees were fired when they refused to sign the policy; two other employees signed the memo and then filed grievances with the EEOC. Altogether, the court found thirteen employees terminated under prejudice, and of those thirteen terminated, fourteen non-Latina/o employees replaced them.

In the case of *EEOC v. Premier Operator Services*, a number of insights were gleaned. First, that the restriction to only speak Spanish to the customers and outside of the building was a discriminatory spatial policy: "The magistrate judge in *Premier Operator Services* pointed out that, under an ability-to-comply standard, '[A] black employee could not challenge a rule requiring the use of separate bathrooms and drinking [fountains]; [and] an Orthodox Jew could not challenge a rule forbidding the wearing of head coverings'" (Colón, 2002, p. 146). Second, that prejudiced behavior "is more often the result of animosity toward the underlying characteristic that an ethnic minority exhibits, than of the literal fact of country of national origin" (Colón, 2002, p. 248).

EEOC v. Premier demonstrates that race and ethnicity in telephony *determine* the ways in which users access technology. For Western technological culture, the telephone was a medium that could buffer or bridge Spanish in xenophobic, "English only" spaces. However, away from the telephone or cord board, that technology as a buffer to Whiteness was also moderated by policy.

The Latina women I interviewed spoke Spanish with their immediate families and friends, but they spoke English without an accent at the cord board to English-speaking customers. There was also a historical precedent for telephone operator harassment of anyone with a Southern accent that the customer perceived as African American or anyone with a Spanish accent (Green, 2001). Race and ethnicity are defined in proximity to technology. In the case of telephony, the telephone and cord board were both a buffer for Whiteness—acting as an acceptable medium for Spanish in English-only spaces—*and* as a harbinger of social anxieties around the increasingly integrating society of African Americans, Latina/os, and Asian Americans in previously White-only workplaces.

How do we account for the underrepresented Latina in information technology fields, especially when considering the lack of diversity in internet start-up companies that now dominate the political economy? While the 1972 EEOC-AT&T consent decree made historic changes to open up the largest private jobs sector to underrepresented people, the historical record on how Latinas were made a part of this three-year process is sparse. Because the case disregarded Latinas—considered only as consumers and "language minorities" and by national origin—the history of Latina involvement in the EEOC-AT&T hearings requires recovery. Despite lengthy academic works published around the *EEOC v. AT&T* case, nuanced records on the Latina experience are widely neglected.

Embedded within the proceedings to include underrepresented people, racial and gendered politics intertwine into the timeline of telecommunications (de la Peña, 2010, p. 921). Further academic work must recognize where Latinas have become employed in technological labor and their impact on the development of information technologies and underlying support of the internet today. Latinas' history in telecommunications must be contextualized by the events that took place during the affirmative action legislations of the 1960s and 1970s. To move Latinas out of the "invisible minority" category, a history built on their own stories must intervene.

3

LATINAS ON THE LINE

Following the civil rights and affirmative action movements of the previous decade, the private and public employment sector in the 1970s saw an influx of Latinas in telecommunications. Now entering retirement age, Latina information workers have been employed in telecommunications for decades, seeing firsthand the divestment of U.S. industries and reinvestment into the private sector, the outsourcing of jobs overseas, and the rapid change of information technologies. Experiencing lifelong careers in corporations at the center of the neoliberal political economy and global labor policies, Latina information workers provide a significant case study in the construction and dissonance of telecommunication information workers in the private sector.

This chapter seeks to understand how Latinas experience the IT sector and the information, technology, and socioeconomic structures of these industries. Specifically, this chapter examines the critical approaches to information technologies that Latinas are already engaging with in their everyday work. Although Latinas approached technology, telecommunications, and the political economy with a critical eye, they did not consciously consider their approach to their labor a "critique." The resulting interpretation of these women's comments as a critical Latinx technology studies is my own. I began with a larger sample size that extended to Latina/os around Southern California and narrowed by interviews and time to these five women because of their long-term experience in telecommunications, valuing the depth of the field they had experienced throughout their lifetimes.

The participants' accounts describe unnamed contradictions, wrestling with the criticisms of the private sector's implementation of neoliberalism. Latinas were included in telecommunications and the neoliberal project because of their difference and were inhibited through methods of surveillance and limited upward mobility in technology-heavy fields. Lower-level Latina employees describe their work as being highly surveilled and having to handle large workloads in a hostile environment; they were further restricted by the information technologies in their workplaces.

BIOGRAPHIES OF FRICTION

The tensions in these interviews are best described as "frictions," advanced by the internal migrations experienced in telecommunications. Friction, according to Anna Lowenhaupt Tsing (2005), arises from global connections of contemporary capitalism developed out of the increasing international trade of the past two decades. Tsing further expands on frictions as being similar to Hall's (1991) work on difference, a necessary element to the larger projects at hand. She writes, "Speaking of friction is a reminder of the importance of interaction in defining movement, cultural form, and agency. Friction is not just about slowing things down. Friction is required to keep global power in motion" (p. 6). One of the key sources of friction expressed by interviewees is the internal migration around the Greater Los Angeles area that defines information workers' lives in telecommunications. "Friction" allows for the uneasy contradictions, the unsettled ideologies in my interviews with Latinas in telecommunications. The disturbed stasis of telecommunications companies becomes the underlying causation of mobility and immobility that organizes information workers' bodies. Cheah asserts that these recognitions include subjects both mobilized and immobilized by globalization (2013, p. 86). For some, such as Maria and Monica, the movement is a daily part of their work. For others, such as Gloria, internal migration happened yearly, when her office was shut down or relocated to another part of Los Angeles. Latina information workers find themselves in forced mobility that is simultaneously liberating and constraining.

These accounts reflect constant changes in job descriptions, information technologies, and geographical location. They are consistent with Cameron McCarthy et al.'s observations on the neoliberal subject's mobility: "The post-welfare state subject is positioned as socially and economically mobile" (2011, p. 10). While Latina information workers' histories enabled crucial analysis of technology and capitalism, their career timelines indicated the constant state/strain of change in telecommunications.

Three of the women I interviewed worked under the Bell system for various lengths and periods of their lives. My first research collaborator is Monica,[1] a second-generation Mexican[2] woman born in Los Angeles in 1952 who has lived in California her whole life. Monica received her high school diploma and attended a community college during her first years at the phone company. Monica worked at Pacific Bell from 1970 to 1982, first as a telephone operator before moving on to various information tasks such as data processing, mail delivery, and payroll records. Though she often performed complex tasks that included feeding data tape into supercomputers' processing systems, Monica was marked as a lower-level employee brought into the Bell system as a part of affirmative action regulations.

Sandra is a Costa Rican woman, born in Atenas, Costa Rica, who moved to California in 1964. She worked for AT&T from 1972 to 1987. She started as a clerk, binding cables manually by adding "feet" to attach the cables. She was then transferred to the furniture department, where she took inventory of materials. After the furniture department, Sandra worked in personal records, amending employee information cards to add "race" into the files. From there, she was transferred to the transportation unit, where she manually entered billing codes into the computers. She used a dial phone to transfer data to San Francisco, using microfilms to find the codes.

Maria is a Mexican woman born and raised in San Pedro, California. She began work at Pacific Bell in 1973 and has remained there to this day, though it is now known as AT&T. Maria began working at Pacific Bell immediately after receiving a high school diploma. She began as a telephone operator, answering calls and transferring customers using phone books. As an operator, Maria used the cord board, a headset, and a plug. Maria transferred to messenger services in Inglewood after two years; she worked there for five years delivering loose mail, equipment, boxes, and cases throughout Pacific Bell. After messenger services, Maria became a facility technician in Huntington Park, a position she still holds. As a facility technician, she provides technical services to landlines around the Los Angeles region at four different offices: San Pedro, Wilmington, Torrance, and Lomita.

Gloria is a second-generation Hispanic and American Indian who has lived in Los Angeles her whole life. After attending one semester of college, she was hired in 1978 as a cord board operator at General Telephone and Electronics, an independent telephone company. Gloria's job was subsumed under Traffic Service Position System (TSPS) as phone companies moved away from cord board operators to automatic systems. In the 1980s, Gloria's job returned to GTE, which merged with Atlantic Bell in the 1990s to become Verizon, where Gloria presently works in general customer service.

Lorraine, who is discussed in chapter 5, has a similar story. She is a second-generation Mexican American and was born and raised in Wilmington in Southern California. Lorraine finished high school and then went back to study business management at the University of Phoenix while she was working for GTE. She moved from telephone operator to manager during her thirty-nine-year-long career and saw the company change from GTE to Verizon, and finally to Frontier.

These biographies of friction set the stage for the experience of internal migration through Greater Los Angeles, conflicting opinions about the welfare state versus the merit system, hypercontrolled bodies through information technologies' surveillance, race and gender analysis of telecommunications, and telecommunications' intimacy. What results is a complex analysis of belonging to, and being separate from, telecommunications.

Internal Migration

The internal migration theme common in the narrative of technological freedom is contingent on the geographic manipulation and immobility of Latina information workers, subject to the will of the telecommunication companies. Maria described the locations that she might visit in a workday: "I take a lot of overtime, and I work in these four offices local to me: San Pedro, Wilmington, Torrance, and Lomita. They're probably six miles away at time, but the service tech will put in a ticket, and I'll have to drive to the offices, and it's not occupied. If they call us, we have to go."[3]

The more a work location changes, the higher the level of stress expressed among the employees. For Gloria, the internal migration phenomenon led to a resentful work environment. However, Gloria transferred the interoffice tensions to individual problems, in sync with the neoliberal narrative:

> I mean, there's women there that don't want to work. I go, "There's a ton of people that want to work, and you don't want to work. You're here, groaning about the work. Go home, retire, and make room for somebody who needs the job." I'm at that point where you get sick of the grumbling. You have to be more grateful, especially nowadays. If you're not grateful for what the Lord has given you—a job, a good-paying job. We all have food on the table. Granted, we all had to move again. It's the move; it's a constant moving. But if you look at my history, it's a constant movement.[4]

Gloria was especially apt to intertwine the trajectory of her career with her personal and spiritual life, relating the parallels of growing up with GTE, a telephone company that started out local and became Verizon.

Telecommunications information work is intricately connected to the larger global economy, and the impacts are felt firsthand, with little room for agency. Gloria spoke of internal migration as a phenomenon that endangered her work but was necessary for "survival." She discussed internal office closures due to mergers and consolidations:

> GLORIA: But subsequently what I've learned now, this change, this is where I work now in Long Beach. Because I went to Pomona; from Downey, they moved us from Pomona, from Pomona to Long Beach. You don't stay stagnant at the phone company. Every office I've worked at has closed.
>
> INTERVIEWER: Did it ever feel like there was a fear to lose the job?
>
> GLORIA: When Whittier was closing, if we didn't find transfers, we would have lost our jobs.
>
> INTERVIEWER: Did you know anyone who had lost their jobs?
>
> GLORIA: Most people found transfers because transfers were being pooled, but it's dog-eat-dog now. I mean, back then most people found jobs if you wanted one. There were a lot of openings back then, and that was in the '90s, and that was when Whittier closed. Then we went to Downey, and they were remodeling Downey and getting all these apartments in there. It was nice. Then they changed to Verizon, and you know Verizon is into consolidation, and that's where you start . . .

When the FCC broke up AT&T, Sandra found herself concerned for her own job's security, although ultimately, she chose her preferred company: "It was two months after I started working in transportation. We were kind of scared because we didn't know where we would end up. They asked us, Where do you want to be? Do you want to be at Pac Bell or General Electric?"⁵

Working outdoors with manual and technological skills is associated with freedom. But the shifting ownership, titles, and geographic location of the companies induced individual stress and interpersonal tension among employees. While Latina information workers adjust to these fluid conditions to keep their job security, the internal migrations scripted by telecommunications are parallel with the challenges and pleasures of skilled labor, therefore disrupting working conditions. Internal migrations augment the contradictory experiences of neoliberalism, resulting in both liberating and confined aspects of information labor. Latina information workers indicate that the displeasure of internal migrations is a point of fracture in the workplace and disturbs "buying into" the neoliberal model that expands telecommunications.

Latina information workers describe the horizontal and vertical mobility experienced during their decades-long careers with information technologies. I use *mobility* as a neutral term, not always denoting an increase in wages or status, but describing the frequent changes in technology and skills that come with the job in major telecommunications companies. Gloria defined this mobility in terms of geographic changes around the Greater Los Angeles region, as well as with merging corporations in constant flux:

> Then we had to choose. Once they were going to close that office, the cord board, and make it computerized, we had to choose where we were going to go. And a friend of mine goes, "Let's go to Mar Vista." I said, "OK." I didn't know where Mar Vista was, but . . . then I went to Mar Vista as a TSPS [Traffic Service Position System] operator. Then when I transferred out of there as a customer service rep in Torrance, then I went to offline support in Whittier. Then they were closing the Whittier office, so we had to look for transfers, so that's when I went to Downey, to assignment.
>
> And during this time, when I first started, the phone company was called General Telephone. And between there and when I

became a rep somewhere in the '80s, they changed to GTE. So they were GTE until . . . let's see, I went to Downey in the '90s, maybe late '90s. They merged with Atlantic Bell, and they became Verizon.

Monica remembers her mobility as vertical and identified how the job and wages improved as she moved up in floors at Pacific Bell. She also notes the changes in technologies, which grew more advanced as she moved upward:

It was one of the main hubs of doing accounting. I went from doing that into the mailroom. So what we did was take all the people's accounting records. And they needed to go to different areas, different places. So we would separate them sometimes with a . . . I think it was called a decollator, because the paper needed to be pulled apart, because the paper came in reams and reams and rows and rows of paper that were almost attached, you know? And then you would separate them, and then send them off to next door, to where they were going to go. And it was seven stories, so we had jobs that needed to be delivered to the other floors as well. Again, I was there for a short time and it was weird to me that it was seven stories, but the higher you went up in the floor, the better the job got. So you started in the mailroom, and then I went to the fourth floor, which was actually the computers there.

Participants' lives were often formed around the practices of Bell as well as greater socioeconomic shifts. Wrapped together into the enjoyment of work and the potential for upward mobility was a larger criticism of the neoliberal economy, which the interviewees indicated impacted their quality of life.

Information Technology Skills and Surveillance

The "freedom" component of neoliberalism is significant because it is often used to describe access to information technologies, but it also inhibits the so-called freedom of Latina/o information workers. Steven Doran describes how mobile devices become a tool in the production of neoliberal citizenship: "Being free means being ruled. In this way neoliberal citizenship can be characterized by both the continued pursuit of individual freedom as well as by systems of domination which are becoming increasingly material, invisible, and infrastructural. The neoliberal citizen is thus a paradoxical figure, at once 'free'—that is, governmental power that regulates and manages conduct through the strategic deployment of such freedom" (Doran, 2011, p. 134).

While the neoliberal era has divested access to welfare and state-funded resources, it has accelerated the narrative of freedom through information technologies. Freedom is presented as "the ability to manage the self remotely, unconstrained by geography. In this way, mobility becomes a powerful signifier of freedom of the neoliberal citizen" (Doran, 2011, p. 138). Latinas in telecommunications experienced the liberatory and regulatory practices that frame information technology culture. All the women enjoyed and sought more skilled jobs. However, information technologies were also discussed as suspect, leading to further surveillance in the workplace.

Although many Latinas work in lower-level telecommunications positions, they have often been some of the first in their communities trained in advanced technologies such as computers. Sandra recalled the process of training in the early 1980s, when she learned to assemble computers and used the original DOS program:

> They sent us to special training, starting how to, how can I tell you? The computer was in the bags, we had to take it out and put it together completely and connect it and everything. Then after they taught us the DOS program, how did they call that? . . . It was like a running program. Now it's Windows; it used to be DOS, and Excel, I don't remember which other ones. We had special programs. They started more, the computer programs started more . . . how can I say, more and more . . . we type something in the computer, then they give us the bill already there, and we put the name and everything, and they sent it back to San Francisco. We didn't have to do anything, they just checked.

Sandra's job in billing also led to her utilizing early data-transferring systems over the phone and with microfilm. She described the use of early data-transferring teletype machines that used step-by-step switches to connect distant offices:

> OK, first, they used to send me. . . . Suppose we contracted, we called contractors for moving tables, and they sent us the bills.

So the bills that came to us would send us codes. First, we did it manually and sent it through the mail, then afterward the computers started. Then we had to dial the phone to San Francisco. Now thinking about the technology . . . we had to push a button and the click click click, you could hear that, and you were connected to San Francisco. And they gave us the codes for the labels. So we worked with microfilms, little ones, to find the codes to see if it was invalid or right. So we would send the bill, give it to the supervisor, he would check that and he would sign it, and then we sent it.

Information labor became intentionally de-skilled as technology shifted work from manual to automatic to digital (Green, 2001, p. 25). Sandra described her work with cables as manual until it transitioned to a more sophisticated technology. Once the technology became more advanced, the job was moved to different geographic locations: "I think it was less than a year. After that, it was transferred to Oakland. It was more sophisticated; they took that department up, and it was no longer. I think that they started more with the computers or something more . . . they started doing different things, not manually. For me, everything was manual; we put the maps and added the feet. So I imagined that they changed or completely took out the department."

Maria expressed her feelings of dissonance with how technology had changed her field. She felt frustrated that she had to call overseas for computer support, a service previously provided by local co-workers:

MARIA: [Regarding] the technology, . . . everything is on the computer. They used to physically come over here with us, but now we go to the websites and do whatever we have to do on the computer. All of my work comes out of the computer. Everything is assigned to us, timed.

INTERVIEWER: When did you start on the computer, and when did you start getting timed?

MARIA: Probably the last maybe twelve or thirteen years, we had to start putting in our own time. Learning the computer is probably like thirteen years. It's supposed to be paperless, but it's not. That's probably when they had us doing all that. Right now, the centers that are here and the COs, we have all of the equipment, but it all can be managed by operators back east. Like the service

center, they're all back east. And every time I have trouble with
my computer or on my desktop, I get calls from India, from the
Philippines.

Although the interview participants worked with technology in
their daily lives, they hesitated to trust it completely. Gloria adapted to
technology quickly in order to stay relevant in her work. However, she
distrusted technology: "But the one thing about the phone company
is it's constant movement. And not just in places, but internal. How
things are working, how things are functioning. And that's just how it
is. The technology has taken over. And you either gotta go with it, you
know. I mean there's certain things I don't like to do, like pay my bills
online. I'm still old school because I don't trust every system."

The de-skilling of labor in relation to technology was a common
topic with Maria and Gloria, both employed their entire careers in
phone companies. Maria noticed that skilled training was related to
the interconnection of community among laborers within the phone
companies. Over time, the compartmentalized knowledge of a system
of communication also led to the breakdown of relationships among
her co-workers: "The people are really what made it too. All my good
friends. You know, because it doesn't seem like it's there anymore.
Everybody would help each other. It's not like that anymore. Everybody is out for themselves. Because they depend on certain people to
do certain things. Some people, they are able not to do nothing where
the management still depends on certain people's jobs. So I think it's
going to be like that everywhere."

Lacking the support of new technologies, the acceleration of technology made Maria uncomfortable with her skill level in her new job
description. Although she enjoyed the skills she deployed in her job,
she felt uneasy at the amount of responsibility the new job descriptions required while receiving little training.

Latinas who have worked in telecommunications since the early
1970s experienced the transition of their work from manual to electronic and online as a shift not only in the greater economy but also in
their personal lives. Many Latinas in telecommunications began their
work as manual telephone operators, plugging into a cord board. For
these women, going "online" meant plugging their headsets in and
fielding incoming calls. As Maria explains, "The calls automatically

came in, and . . . our timing was all essential. We had to make so many calls in so many minutes of information. You know, they would time us. And back in that day, we used to use the big phone books and turn the pages. You know the white pages and the yellow pages in a phone book, it was. People that didn't have it at hand. . . . We had our stations and we would plug in, and the call would automatically come through. Often we would get monitored."

Gloria described her first experience with computer training, remembering that her work changed from the manual cord board to computers around 1978:

> We always had training for different things. Customer service was always drilled into you. Constantly training customer service, anything new coming up. But we did have classes on how to use the computers. At first, during the time we're in this office. The way it was set up was you went to different job functions as an online rep. So you were an online rep, then you went to this thing called VAF, and what that was is you more interfaced with the reps. And we had at that time phonemarts, which the customer would go in and place an order, which they would purchase a phone or lease a phone. . . . Different things happen and we got the first computers for that system because it needed the address and stuff. So by staying there I got the first training on the first little computer they brought in to do that work, so it really helped me to do that other stuff. When it came time to do orders, I was a little more comfortable doing what I had to do.

All the participants discussed a wide range of skills, from the mundane and repetitive motions of the telephone operator to early applications of software training. However, their experience with information technologies did not occur in a vacuum but was tied to the larger operations of their companies. Mobility and change are two of the phenomena that arose during these interviews.

TELEPHONY SURVEILLANCE

Among all the interviewees, a critique was present of the shift in the value of labor, the change in technology and skills. This analysis of the larger socioeconomic structure indicates the shifting global economy, the social construction of technology, and the de-skilling of labor. A clear parallel became evident throughout these discussions between the hypersurveilled and monotonous work of the telephone operator, a position in which three interviewees began their work, and the contemporary organization of technology labor within large telecommunications conglomerates.

Dominant tech sector beliefs advocate that technology has an accelerating effect on efficiency and time. Technology as progress is naturalized in the United States as having only positive effects on personal lives, workplaces, and economic growth. Latina information workers identified a distrust of technology because they have seen firsthand their jobs de-skilled, their work overloaded, and their co-worker communities fragmented. While all interviewees identified these negative associations with technology as more recent developments, one interesting phenomenon arose that harkened back to information work of the past, now made almost obsolete. The occupation of the telephone operator, a job where many Latinas began their employment in the phone companies, was described as congruent with present-day information work. The 1970s telephone operators came from a long history of highly surveilled and overworked labor. Operators were subject to decades of physically grueling and surveilled work and often responded with union organizing and activism for better working conditions. Latina information workers found their work in more recent years to be similarly inhospitable. Although they regarded these working conditions as results of the neoliberal era, the similarities to the telephone operator work of the past may resist the "newness" of this phenomenon. The parallel between the telephone operators of the past and today's telecommunications information workers indicates that new formations of neoliberalism are put into action through old models of technological displacement.

The telephone operator position was an entry job for Monica, Gloria, and Maria that led to more skilled, better-paying opportunities. They described this work as highly surveilled, physically tedious, monotonous, and stressful:

> MONICA: When I first got a job there, we wore these black head-
> sets that you see, very, very heavy, and you would put the ear-
> piece over your mouth. You would get one of those, go to a little

cubicle, and you would plug in. And as soon as you plug into a network, calls would start coming in—the 411 calls. At the time they were the directory assistance. And you would answer eight hours a day. . . . You were all to get phone numbers, phone listings. Or if you couldn't, you would get a supervisor. So there were, like, two supervisors on staff all the time.

GLORIA: It's tedious work, and it started to affect, because at that time I was partying a lot. And when you're an operator and you're bored, you seem to party a little harder. So I just needed to do something else.

MARIA: Yes, well, I know I wasn't happy there in operator services. I was almost going to quit. I was just overwhelmed because it was a stressful job. Your hours are staggered, you have to turn on a light if you want to go to the bathroom, and only one person on the floor could go to the bathroom at once. It's really strict and you're constantly monitored.

As technology became automated, the work became de-skilled. Maria indicated that the level of surveillance on her work has greatly increased since technologies such as GPS have developed: "I have a GPS and we have our cell phones too, and I heard we have GPS on our cell phone . . . they monitor our driving all the time and everything seems to be more stricter in the policy."

The de-skilling of labor became a common topic among conversations with Maria and Gloria, who had lifelong careers in phone companies and had not moved into management positions. Gloria's career shifted a number of times by geography and title. She made decisions on where to work based on attempting to keep her technological skill level up, exercising the small amount of agency she was given: "Well, my job in Whittier moved to Florida. Florida took over that function. So jobs going out of state is bad. . . . When we were still GTE, we did everything as one function. When we went to Verizon, they kept Atlantic Bell, how they do things, and they separated job functions: switch and assignment, two different categories. So since I was already doing both, I decided to stay with switch because it's more challenging and I like it."

Because of the decades of insight that the interview participants have had in telecommunications, they identify a clear degradation of their work and skills with information technologies. Though they adapted to the new conditions with resolve, they often identified a general suspicion of technology and its overall effect on community, quality of life, and the well-being of the companies themselves.

RACE AND GENDER

Race and gender were purposefully discussed during these interviews, but with varying results. Sandra, Maria, and Gloria did not believe they experienced discrimination as Latinas in the field, and primarily worked in offices with a majority of Latina/os and African Americans. All the women noted that, with a few exceptions, supervisors were White men.

Latina experiences with telephony, the phone company, and telecommunications occur at the junction where Latina/o identity and race are hashed out. Latina/o racial identity has long been up for debate in the law, the public sphere, and among the Latina/o experience in the United States. When these multiple racial experiences meet with telephony, the telephone becomes the mediator wherein *Latinidad* can be flushed out. Among telephone operators, the telephone cloaks phenotype by presenting only the voice. If a Latina telephone operator spoke without an accent, they were cast as English-speaking telephone operators, able to "pass" as White women.

Gloria felt her workplace had always been a diverse space, although not in supervisory roles: "Yeah it was very diverse, that's one thing [about] GTE. . . . Diversity is one of I think GTE's better strengths. They've always been diverse. . . . When I first started, it seemed like, they had a lot of African American supervisors. I didn't really see any Hispanic higher-ups, but in an operator smaller office, we didn't see that. We went to TSPS [Traffic Service Position Systems], again I think most of the supervisors were White; the high managers were White."

Many negative experiences in the workplace were blamed on individuals' actions rather than linked to race and gender. Gloria and Maria both expressed uncertainty about the nature of discrimination that they ultimately ascribed to individual attitudes rather than race and gender. Gloria told me, "I've had a couple of supervisors that, you know, you didn't want to come out and say, or they hid it well. But then they would do stuff to other people who weren't Hispanic, so I figured it's just them. . . . I always just give people the benefit of the doubt. Since I was a child, I never felt discriminated against for being Hispanic."

Maria also described discrimination as a conflicted experience. While she could not directly identify racial and gendered discrimination, Maria found that her age worked against further opportunities:

> INTERVIEWER: Did you ever feel, as a Latina in this field, like you experienced discrimination?
>
> MARIA: I think I did . . . but I don't know how to put it. Not really; I think it was more about personalities. I don't really feel like I had any discrimination. I think if anything, because I was Latina, I was offered more opportunities. I could have probably advanced more than I felt comfortable to do. And as I'm getting older, my opportunities are getting less and less.

Monica recognized particular experiences in which she felt discriminated against as a Latina in a mostly White workplace. She acknowledged loneliness in the spaces she worked where she was the only Latina: "And I went to, first to become a telephone operator, where our job was to look up phone numbers to the public, but we had to be trained for that. So for two weeks you learn about area codes and counties, location, in color coded books, which were the directories. And it seemed like a simple job, and it was, but it was difficult because there were no other Latinos there at all, so I just felt so out of place."

Monica also recognized that her level of access to more sophisticated information technologies was limited and that White employees had more access to certain technologies, such as a large data processing computer:

> Right, I didn't feel like I accomplished much. I didn't know why I wasn't allowed to go into the big computer center. We were not allowed to go in there, only certain ones. And I wanted to go in there.
>
> Yeah, they were working in there all the time. Changing the wheels, because the computer tapes were massive, you know, the database was huge. And all we would do was get the wheels ready for them. So I didn't feel like . . . I didn't accomplish much of anything in there. . . .
>
> There were White technicians that would go in and out. There were the engineers, the technicians, they were always around. Like

I said, everybody wore a blue coat, and there were a few African American women allowed to put the reels in, but I don't remember any Latino people going in.

One of the most interesting cases among the interviewees was Sandra. Sandra, of all the interviewees, has the most identifiable accent when speaking English, as she had migrated to the United States after high school. She attained her job at Bell by answering an advertisement specifically looking for Spanish speakers after the consent decree was passed. One of Sandra's jobs was to add race to employee data cards. Sandra noted that she never experienced discrimination at Bell. She was certain she was not hired due to affirmative action and that all employees were treated equally at Bell.

Racial and gendered experiences in the Bell system are varied and acknowledged differently by Latina women. While Gloria and Maria had initially acknowledged racism at Bell, they could not specifically identify how, so they quickly changed to a color-blind narrative. Of all the interviewees, only Monica directly identified that race and gender had dictated the organization of the workplace and access to more skilled jobs at Bell.

Telecommunications' Intimacy

The neoliberal contradictions of freedom from government control and U.S. self-determinism are key themes in these histories. Throughout the interview sessions, tension was expressed between the benefits of the preneoliberal welfare state—such as labor unions—and the "merit system," which neglects structural discriminations and promises success through individual hard work. Most of the interview collaborators agreed that the field of telecommunications would not have hired them without affirmative action and the civil rights movements, but they were often torn between the need for workers' rights and self-determination via the merit system. Monica knew she was hired as an immediate consequence of affirmative action:

Well, when I was in high school at the time, the affirmative action movement was going. And this man, out of nowhere, I just remember what he looked like, tall thin man came up to Susie and I, my sister and I. And our first job was working at the high school, and immediately after that, he said to me that there was a job opening at the phone company. And man, we jumped on it. It so happened that I took two more of my Latino friends, but they didn't get the job, and the way I see it is they met their quota with Susie and I. Because I could definitely tell that they were looking for minorities to work there. Because everyone there was White and they had to fill that gap, because you could totally see it.

The opinion of Latina information workers on affirmative action in telecommunications directly contradicts the neoliberal ideology that individual hard work and freedom of corporate enterprise will translate into success. However, this is the site of tension that conflicts with the interview subjects most frequently, rationalized via individual hard work. The interviewees often asserted that the individual is responsible for their own success despite the globalized economic conditions that drive working conditions.

Unions were discussed, both positively and negatively, to varying degrees. Gloria spoke about her union as a necessary element for her own rights, but advocated the neoliberal ideology of "hard work" at all costs:

> You know I work on a computer, and I really like my job now. It makes you think. You have so many different job functions. The way I see my job now is, you have to make yourself . . . what's the word, almost needed. The more you learn you're a valued employee. I work with a union. We're a union. And there's good and bad in that. The good part is that if you're up for a contract, you want to make sure it's fair. I think the bad place in a union is that there are employees who really take for granted their job, they don't work. You know, they go to work and they're not working.

Gloria realized that she must make herself indispensable to be recognized as employable at Verizon while working in customer service, but she also questioned the union's protection for employees. But Maria was concerned that incoming telecommunications information workers were more vulnerable and further de-skilled with the loss of unions. As companies were broken up or merged, telecommunications offices increased work hours and stress levels while reducing benefits. Maria named identity, relocation, and the shift in corporate culture as factors decreasing the quality of her work: "I think every time they changed our name—we were PacBell and then Cingular, now we're AT&T—every time we changed, we got all new procedures. What do you call that, when everything is different, the way you handle everything? . . . Using temps, it's more nonunion. . . . They think it's cost-effective, but actually, we're going a little bit backward. They see it working over there; it's more productive and less money."

Latina information workers are embedded in an impossible paradox of inclusion, recognition, and rugged individualism. These workers recognize their unions (for those who have them) and affirmative action as necessary mediators into private domains. However, they also consciously engage the corporate paradigm of hard work. The contradicting accounts between the welfare state and the merit system point to both an erosion of and an adherence to the overarching utopic promises of neoliberalism and the "information age." Information technologies further deploy neoliberal standards through surveillance and control.

Latina information workers have been engaging in intricate and monotonous technological skills in a constantly changing environment. They identified pleasure in skilled work and chose complex tasks for more enjoyable jobs. However, the trajectory of technological displacement leads Latina information workers further into mundane, automated, and digitized roles, causing them to feel more like a "number" and less like an individual with skills (Green, 2001). While working with information technologies in telecommunications can be pleasurable, the state of controlled surveillance with information technologies creates a rupture with the overarching state of digital capitalism. The promise of freedom and individualism through information technologies for consumers is only accomplished through the confinement of information workers. If information workers are "made" through recognition, Latina telecommunication workers are unraveled through information technologies' control and surveillance.

Each woman articulated her experiences as negative when skills were mundane, and work was monotonous and positive when they were challenged and engaged in complex tasks. These sets of skills were clearly identified as having been more readily available earlier on in their careers, when they had more options to move into various roles in their respective companies. They identified access

to developing their skills in multiple areas of their fields as ben-
eficial, superseded by the rapid change in information technologies
and the frequent shifting of larger corporate mergers and breakups.
This analysis, though not specifically named, is in direct relationship to the shifting economies, globalized labor, and manufacturing practices of the neoliberal period. The interview participants
identified a lack of community, poor management practices, and an
unhealthy work environment as a direct result of these changes.

Latinas in IT, telecommunications, and STEM fields use affect as a
mode of agency in describing their work. Affect, as well as affect theory,
must be engaged as a point where technological skills and embodied
experience meet. Cvetkovich (2012) identifies the affective turn as one
that depathologizes "negative feelings" such as shame, failure, melan-
choly, and depression and identifies these feelings as entwined with positive feelings such as hope and happiness. Validating the feelings expressed
in these technological spaces engages the critical analysis of technologies.
All the women I interviewed had saved old telephones, operator headsets, company books, and other technologies from their workplaces as
artifacts of memory and affect. Allowing technological artifacts into
their personal domestic spaces indicated the pride they took in their
labor, integrating the personal and political (Cvetkovich, 2012, p. 177).

All the women interviewed noted that supervisors were mostly
White, while lower-level employees were more diverse. Monica attributed intense discrimination in her workplace to her difference. This
may be due to two reasons. First, Monica began working in telecommunications earlier than the other women interviewed. She clearly
identified affirmative action and the civil rights movement as playing
a part in her integration into these workspaces and found herself as
one of the only Latinas working as a telephone operator in the early
1970s. Intense instances of marginalization seemed to cause some
Latinas to more openly recognize their experiences of discrimination,
though not without some self-blame. By the mid-1970s, due to the
affirmative action movement by the EEOC, many sectors of manufacturing and customer service had integrated more diverse employees
into telecommunications. The interviewees described these diverse
spaces as creating a more enjoyable environment. They often engaged
the idea of "The Family," an early motto of the Bell system, as a time
before neoliberal restructuring, when these sectors provided a better

quality of life. Interpersonal tensions arose with the de-skilling of labor and the decentralization of workspaces.

For Latina information workers in telecommunications, neoliberal subject formations meet and diverge in contradictory spaces. Latina information workers' narratives challenge the story of telecommunications by expressing a relationship of "friction" to their work. Latina information workers were hired into a limited sector within telecommunications through affirmative action, finding themselves in what Tsing describes as "sticky engagements" (2005, p. 6) that keep global power in motion. Within Latina information workers' oral histories are paradoxes that work with and against the neoliberal formulations of capitalism, meritocracy, and technology as progress.

Intensified models of global capitalism and information technology surveillance have disrupted Latina information workers' sense of belonging in telecommunications. The decades of experience of Latina information workers in telecommunications unveil two conclusions: (1) that contemporary forms of neoliberalism erode its own sense of belonging to corporate spaces and (2) that telecommunications in the United States might be taking on new formulations of hypercontrol with fewer benefits of inclusion and recognition (Amar, 2013). This work suggests that new configurations of capitalism are motivated by old and continuous techniques of technological displacement. Latina information workers' accounts of telecommunications, information technologies, and the larger state of capitalism are crucial in identifying points of rupture in the political economy. These interviews point to an opening in the breakdown of the belief in capitalism and the need for new labor organizing in information technology sectors that speak to the vulnerabilities identified by Latina information workers. In the next chapter, I look further into the topic of "belonging" to the "family" structure of telecommunications.

4

WE WERE FAMILY

Bell recruited Latina workers just in time for the liberalizing economy and the breaking down of the "Bell family." The Bell family, once a method for mobilizing against trade unions, was one of the "benefits" that was whittled down during the neoliberal period, and it mainly disappeared after AT&T's divestiture. This chapter explores how the implementation and disappearance of the Bell family impacted Latina information workers. During the 1970s, Latinas in Southern California experienced a variety of "family" systems, from their cultural familial expectations to family structures shaped by the Chicano rights movement, which influenced the final proceedings of the consent decree, to the Bell family structure, which was intensely implemented among female employees. With the dissolving of the Bell family, Latinas found themselves at a loss for community and job training.

The Bell family became one site of formation and dissolution of the heteronormative family structures within Latinas' personal and work lives. Latinas in telecommunications were recruited into the Bell family during a transition time, in which the benefits from the previous century were dissolving.

THE BELL FAMILY, CONSTRUCTED

Latina information workers' memories of the Bell family are ones of nostalgia for the preneoliberal era and for benefits that were put in place to deter unionism, solidify the type of nationalism that joined AT&T with the larger U.S. family, and build White segregated familial ties. By the time these women joined Bell, only some of those benefits remained in place. After the breakup of the Bell system through divestiture and years of the liberalized economy, those diminished benefits were longed for. For example, the workplace would never stabilize; rather, constant change and mobility became the norm. For these women, there were three common themes regarding the idea of "the family": (1) the "Bell family" of old, foregrounded by a racialized system of Whiteness, which they entered into and were ineligible for due to their difference; (2) the traditional discourse of the Latina/o and Chicano family, which shaped Latina inclusion into telecommunications; (3) Latinas' personal and private family lives, inevitably overlapping with telecommunications.

The Bell family was used to diverge with unions and create a family of customers and employees alike. After the world wars, the family system was also used to reinstate nationalism and an affinity for AT&T. Three shifts in the Bell ecosystem disintegrated the ideas of and attempts at the "family": the integration of African American women in the operator workforce, the implementation of divestiture in the 1980s, and the slow dissolution of the preneoliberal antiunion tools in exchange for a more globalized workforce. Where do Latinas fit into this structure? Latinas were brought into the Bell family to experience its final benefits, witness its dissolution, and express a nostalgic longing for the preglobalized and liberalized economy. The remnants of the Bell family have also become deeply entwined in Latina information workers' personal lives, finding their way into their homes and personal collections and acting as physical anchors to a time in the telephone company when they belonged to the Bell family (Green, 2001).

The implementation of the Bell family began in the early nineteenth century but especially arose during the first World War. In 1877, the first operator exchanges were being installed in major cities across the country. At this time, operators were mostly young boys who were known for their impatience and roughhousing (Brooks, 1975, p. 66). Bell hired young middle-income women and replaced the image of the male telephone operator with that of a nurturing position rooted in White femininity. Not only was the job of the telephone operator created through rigid adherence to gender roles, but the representation, implementation, and national discourse of the telephone also maintained a performance of gender. The national image of the telephone was one that eased the burden of women's domestic lives:

farm wives' isolation was now remediated with the use of the telephone, urban wives were saving time on shopping, and the institution of the "call girl" was invented (Brooks, 1975, p. 94). The first story about the telephone was a conversation between two women, written by Mark Twain, and the 1909 *Lippincott's Monthly* accused the telephone of building a habit among women to gossip "for the exchange of twaddle between foolish women. . . . It has become an unmitigated domestic curse" (Brooks, 1975, p. 118). In the early twentieth century, White women telephone operators were represented as performing a public service to their nation. The rural operator became an image of a central messaging center, positioned as almost "heroic" in bringing the news of floods and fires to the country (Brooks, 1975). These were representations of White women among imagined communities that made up the "nation." Women of color were not represented in examples of telephone use.

In pre–World War I America, the White female telephone operator represented a soothing caretaker role. In 1918, Bell publicists presented the female operator as the "most economical servant—the only flesh and blood servant many telephone users could afford. The idealization of the female telephone operator drew on conventional gender stereotypes of women as eager to please" (John, 2010, p. 385). Company paternalism further drafted and implemented this gendered labor. The Bell Company placed itself as the telephone operator's guardian. A recruiting brochure for the Chicago Telephone Company announced that it provided "the parental care of a far-seeing monopoly" (Norwood, 1990, p. 48).

During the war, the family was first discussed in conjunction with those soldiers overseas who served in the "Signal Corps," employees of Bell in the newly developed arm of the military that represented communications. The Bell family was depicted in tandem with the United States as a nation. *The Telephone Review* during this time reified the allegiance to Bell and the United States by representing the soldiers and employees overseas and the importance of communications in World War I:

> It is this indispensable need which the telephone only can supply that makes the service, both at home and "over there," so important in "winning the war." When we remember what Americans have

done in the development of telephone, and when we recall that twenty-five hundred of our co-workers are enlisted in the Signal Corps, U.S.R., just because they are trained and competent members of the great Bell family, there is no room left for doubt that all who are in any way connected with this industrial art are giving the country the best service they can possibly render in proportion as they are putting forth their best efforts in their work. (New York Telephone Company, 1917, p. 309)

The early twentieth century brought the rise of labor unions. The first union, the International Brotherhood of Electrical Workers, signed a formal agreement with Bell in 1900. White female telephone operators, despite the exclusion of women in unions, formed an autonomous department within the IBEW in 1918. Green (2001) finds that during the 1920s, Bell system president Theodore N. Vail and managers nationwide organized around the idea of "employee associations"— company unions to "curb the operators' militancy and give control they needed to improve and restore the system" (p. 137): The Bell system's concept of the family was used to substitute and displace independent trade unionism. In the Bell family, employees—especially White women telephone operators—were meant to be submissive. Their participation in organizing unions resisted this narrative of submission. These association meetings functioned as "union" meetings: recording minutes, holding elections, and providing a space for free discussions about general topics but without an avenue to change working conditions. In 1923, 60 percent of association representatives were supervisors and 40 percent were operators, clerks, and other lower-level employees, demonstrating the distribution of power in these "unions": "As members of the 'Bell system family,' employee acquiescence and submission served larger goals related to rates or public relations, new technology, and the general high profits provided by keeping wages low" (Green, 2001, p. 144). The associations assisted in enforcing low-wage policies in which they could pay operators the lowest amount of wages for a larger load of work and determined operators' wages by merit.

As telephone operators joined labor unions nationwide or creating unions when they were denied membership into White male unions, Bell management further developed the Bell family through such nonunion benefits as "employee associations," cozy restrooms, and free lunch, in order to curb operators from leaving the building altogether: "To promote employee loyalty and increase work efficiency, Bell management established retiring rooms and cafeterias for telephone operators during the early twentieth century. . . . A telephone exchange retiring room was supervised by a woman known as the 'matron' or 'operators' quarters supervisor.' Bell management, intent on presenting the company as a 'family,' envisioned her as a 'mother-substitute' who typified the 'human side of the telephone business'" (Norwood, 1990, p. 49).

The "family" was implemented in all spaces of work. The matrons overseeing the telephone operators functioned as surveilling management who stood behind the switchboards, but they were also positioned by Bell as motherly figures: "Management imposed a harsh discipline over the operators at the switchboard. . . . Even during their brief rest breaks, the operators were under the careful scrutiny of older women called *matrons*, charged with curbing boisterous conduct. Norwood (1990) writes about how management explicitly referred to these matrons as 'mothers' and to the operators as 'their girls.' The operators, however, were more likely to view the matrons as police officers, surveilling their movements while standing behind and above them while they sat at the switchboard" (Norwood, 1990, p. 12).

As a response to the labor unions gaining ground after World War I, the "family" circulated as an idea that would last through the 1970s and resonate among employees of Bell/AT&T by way of the Employees' Benefit Fund. About the "family," Vail said, "We have felt more than ever that we are just one big family with every employee having a seat at the family table" (Green, 2001, p. 137). Employee associations disseminated the ideology of the "family" and the importance of employees' obligations and contributions to the family's prosperity in the post–World War I years. Bell managers, and particularly President Vail, directed the notion of the "family" as recommitting loyalty to the nation and recommitting the nation's loyalty to AT&T, thus intertwining the AT&T family and the nationalist family (Green, 2001).

The employee associations were discussed by Bell management at conferences: "Once the majority of employees accepted associations, the Bell system began to institute the strategies that had been formulated in conferences. At these conferences . . . men discussed specific plans designed for what they perceived to be women's peculiar sentimentality. The plans incorporated and reinforced patronizing, chauvinistic, and condescending myths about women" (Green, 2001, p. 146).

At those conferences, management planned to reinforce gender expectations of White women operators via sentiment and sympathy, attempting to place White women in the familial role of the quiet woman who did not require high wages: "Bell system officials fostered this image of the quiet suffering 'ladies,' whose compliant personalities identified them as a stereotypical and homogenized group who could receive 'a different kind of wage treatment'" (Green, 2001, p. 147).

Within the employee associations, representatives were elected to discuss wages and working conditions but did not possess the power to change anything. The associations also enforced low-wage policies and placed operators on a "merit"-based wage schedule, avoiding raises mandated by their own union contracts. Despite this, membership in the Bell family still held prestige for operators because of its racial homogeneity. Racial homogeneity framed the Bell family's structure and determined the family as "middle" class. Telephone operators' membership in this family served racial hierarchies and aided Bell in accomplishing larger goals of public relations and higher profits (Green, 2001, pp. 144–148).

The Chicano Family, Inherited

Multiple national events in the 1960s and early 1970s contextualize the opening of telecommunications to minorities, as well as the ongoing exclusion of Latinas in information technology spaces. The political, social, racial, gender, and labor history preceding the consent decree is significant to the *EEOC v. AT&T* case. In post–World War II America, structural racisms were challenged to include previously marginalized groups, especially impacting Latinas in the United States. After the Civil Rights Act of 1964, the 1960s continued to be a tumultuous time of activism for Latinas in multiple sectors of U.S. society, which was recently confronted by the Chicano rights movement. In 1968, East Los Angeles student walkouts and community meetings indicated the discontent among the Mexican community regarding the treatment of Latina/os in schools. Latina/o culture developed political momentum with literature, poems, and film. Street theater was performed to urban populations on the subject of the labor conditions of migrant workers, led by charismatic leaders Cesar Chavez and Dolores Huerta. On August 29, 1970, between twenty and thirty thousand Chicanos marched through East Los Angeles in the National Chicano Moratorium March against the War in Vietnam (Oropeza, 2000).

A disregard for Latina leadership within the Chicano rights movement, in parallel with overlooking intersectional identities in the feminist movement, became a source of political isolation for Latinas/ Chicanas. Chicanas[1] identified reform as a change to all forms of social inequality, insisting upon an intersectional approach to social change. But Chicanas within the Chicano movement were relegated to traditional gender roles. Resisting U.S. nationalism, *Chicanismo* relied on a cultural nationalist masculinist ideology. Chicanas were positioned in "caretaker" roles in the larger movement and were accused of breaking up the "family" when challenging *Chicanismo* with feminist critiques (Segura and Pesquera, 1998, p. 106). Chicanas also resisted White feminism because of its tendency to overlook race-ethnic, class, and cultural divisions between women, claiming instead to unite as "sisters" (Pesquera and Segura, 1998). White U.S. feminists approached race and class inequality as issues from the previous decade's civil rights movements, leaving Chicanas excluded from both groups. Omitted by these social movements, Latinas were designated as peripheral laborers and activists.

The *Unique Competence* report, though detailed on the lack of Latina/o employees within AT&T, at no point defines the unique discriminations against Latina/os. *A Unique Competence* overlooked specific genders until the last page of the report, ending with the famous poem "I Am Joaquin" by Chicano activist Rodolfo Gonzales:

I am Joaquin / Lost in a world of confusion / Caught up in the whirl of an Anglo society, / Confused by the rules, / Scorned by attitudes, / Suppressed by manipulation, / And destroyed by modern society. / My fathers have lost the economic battle, / And won the fight for cultural survival.

In a country that has wiped out all my history, stifled all my pride / In a country that has placed a different indignity upon my ancient burdens. Inferiority is the new load . . . (Papers of Marjorie Stockford, 1971, p. 289)

For Chicana feminists and scholars, "I Am Joaquin" represented the empowered Chicano, an existential Latino male hero who faced Anglo-dominated spaces as a revolutionary figure. Chicana scholar Angie Chabram-Dernersesian (1992) analyzes the implications of "I Am Joaquin" alongside similar cultural productions of the Chicano rights movement. Chabram-Dernersesian (1992) argues that the Chicano male literary subjects, written in the o/os linguistic qualifier, "subsume the Chicana into a universal ethnic subject that speaks with the masculine instead of the feminine and embodies itself into a Chicano male" (p. 82). Without the consideration of Latinas' needs as information workers and customers within the preliminary report, *A Unique Competence* dichotomized Latina identity into the "gender first" ideology foregrounded by NOW and the male-centric Chicano rights movement's priorities that "I Am Joaquin" performed. *A Unique Competence* identified discriminations against Spanish-surnamed people, but it continued the invisibility of Latinas by leaving them unnamed. With "I Am Joaquin" concluding the report, Latino men were the default "invisible minority."

To understand the Bell family that Latinas entered into is to also understand the formation of the national "Chicano" family, as it greatly influenced the consent decree's resolution. Chicano history begins with the conquest of the United States over the Southwest in 1848 and the signing of the Treaty of Guadalupe Hidalgo. Since that time, Latina/os were subject to segregation, lynching, state violence, and labor exploitation (González and Fernández, 1998, p. 93). *Chicano* and *Chicana* became terms that marked a new political identity of Latina/os in the United States. The Chicano rights movement was the outcome of identifying with these histories and cultural nationalisms. Throughout the 1960s, Chicano rights movements on the West Coast were motivated by the mythical cultural idea of "Aztlán," a geographic place of Aztec origin believed to be in the southwestern United States. Aztlán acted as a rallying point of cultural nationalism for Chicano activists responding to racial exploitation (Klor de Alva, 1998, p. 71). Within the ranks of the Chicano rights movement, Latinas—identifying themselves as Chicana—were often pigeonholed into stereotyped gender roles and excluded from leadership (Blackwell, 2011, p. 31).[2] Richard Rodriguez's seminal work *Next of Kin* (2009) explores the Chicana and Chicano family, noting that "if there is a single issue almost always at stake in Chicano/a cultural politics since the Chicano movement of the 1960s and 1970s, it is the family in some shape, form, or fashion" (p. 2). The Chicano family framework both reinstitutes gendered patriarchal normative roles and extends them into telecommunications but also resists U.S. nationalism, leaving Latinas in telecommunications disidentified in both the Chicano family and the Bell family.

Within the Chicano rights movement, women were often placed in gendered roles as mothers or caretakers. When Chicanas raised issues about patriarchy within the movement, they were often labeled as traitors or White (Segura and Pesquera, 1998, p. 196). Many women of color organized their own "feminisms" and were leaders in these movements, where multiple strands of feminisms intervened in U.S. politics (Blackwell, 2011). Latina/Chicana feminists organized around their intersectional needs through political action, community organizing, academic scholarship, and artistic expression (Ruiz and Sánchez Korrol, 2005). Latinas entering into the Bell system during the 1970s had a long history in the United States as gendered and sexualized subjects, activists, and underrepresented laborers.

The preliminary filings of *A Unique Competence* framed the oncoming proceedings of *EEOC v. AT&T*, opening up the largest company of private-sector employees to underrepresented people at the onset of job loss in previously flourishing industries. The discourse around the inclusion of Latina/os in the subsequent EEOC report, *A Unique Competence*, favored Latino men's recruitment into the Bell system. The hegemonic disposition of Latinas within the Chicano rights movement set the precedent for oversight within ethnic legal rights organizations.

The Family and Visual Representations in the Phone Company

After the 1973 consent decree, Latinas recognized themselves increasingly in AT&T employee handbooks, human resources video trainings on diversity, and eventually in AT&T commercials. The family was a popular trope in how AT&T presented itself before divestiture. In the 1970s, job handbooks were changing to reflect the growing diversity in the company. Images of women and men of color and White women frequented the pages, performing all levels of tasks within the phone company. Latinas noted that after the 1982 consent decree—a consent decree that led to divestiture—was a time of disorientation, when the AT&T family broke apart and these women lost a community that held strong ties and value.

In the 1970s and 1980s, there was growing representation of the "Latina/o family." Products such as Proctor and Gamble, AT&T, Sears, McDonald's, Colgate-Palmolive, and Johnson & Johnson all began marketing on the assumption that Latina/o families were lower income but had larger families and needed more products (Dávila, 2001, p. 94). AT&T, using the advertising company the Bravo Group, would often represent the Latina/o identity as one aligned with family, identity, and nostalgia. Dávila's analysis of commercials from the 1970s and 1980s found that it was common to show Latina/o families in kitchens with women cooking and taking care of children. Multigenerational households were also frequently visualized. Dávila (2001) describes an AT&T ad for the auto-redial feature: "It depicted a nervous boyfriend asking permission to marry his girlfriend. . . . The ad was based on the view that Hispanics have good family values and a religious orientation" (p. 95). AT&T used a trope of contrasting traditional Mexican and Latin American historical images—such as pyramids, which were meant to evoke nostalgia and homeland—with contemporary life in the United States. In AT&T commercials of the '70s, '80s, and '90s, the telephone was demonstrated as a way to connect the "familia" across countries and continents. Indeed, AT&T's products were a perfect medium for their visualized customer base, which they represented as journeying from their homelands of chicken buses and pyramids to their new, middle-income, tech-updated lives in the United States (Dávila, 2001, p. 103).

The "Latin Look" has long been established in U.S. marketing as a social construction that promotes the idea that Latina/os are "homogeneous entities" (Dávila, 2001, p. 42). This homogeneity encourages anti-Blackness in denying that Black people can be Latina/os and anti-indigeneity in disallowing Latina/os to be represented as too indigenous. The outcome is a "rigid raced and gendered visual discourse of the 'Latin Look' and the manner it reflects as well as it impacts popular conceptualizations of Latina/o Identity" (Cepeda, 2016, p. 349). The "Latin Look" has been built into media advertising toward the Hispanic market, noting that the "generic Hispanic" is represented as having olive skin and straight dark hair (Dávila, 2001, p. 111). The olive-skin "mixed" look in phone company commercials projects back further into the idea of the *cosmic race*, constructed by Mexican philosopher Jose Vasconcelos, and discourse commonly found in Latin American nationalist ideologies. The cosmic race idealized postcolonial Latina/os for being less indigenous but not quite fully European: "As opposed to Anglo-Americans, whose injustice and inhuman materialism had led them to exterminate or exclude indigenous populations from their 'civilization,' Latin Americans had kindly 'mated' with them and assimilated them into a new culture where 'inferior' and 'lower' races could be improved and ameliorated" (Dávila, 2001, p. 111).

The outcome of the Latin Look in phone company advertising is that it is the acceptable caricature of a Latina/o person whose phenotype, lack of accent, and conservative family values are *the* qualifiers for technological compatibility. A Latina/o person making a call to their family, from the United States to their country of origin, is represented as technologically sophisticated *because of* their ideal Latina/o identity. Thus the entryway to using developing technologies becomes the ideal colonized Latina/o identity, improving family values and contributing to consumption in the United States. The telephone was also used as a technology that buffers the ethnicity and culture that is usually resisted in the United States. The telephone acts as a *filter* that distills *Latinidad* from undesirable traits: brownness, speaking Spanish first, being indigenous and Latina/o, and being undocumented. In AT&T ads, the telephone becomes a conduit for desirable *Latinidad*, transposed through telephony. The telephone also conveys the ability to keep some members of Latina/o communities *over there*, in their home country. While Spanish can be spoken through the telephone, it acts as a buffer for keeping English first beyond that technology.

"We Were Family": Latina Nostalgia and Memory

When I asked Maria how these liberalizing policies impacted her work, she remembered the "family" structure as one that correlated with better labor skills and relationships among co-workers. She said, "We used to be a big family. We knew the plant service center. We knew the techs out in the field. Constant work with the same people. And now the way they're distributing the work, loading out the trouble, it's really different."[3]

For these women, the family structure wasn't remembered for its gendered roles or racial segregation but for information laborers having interrelated relationships and physical proximity to one another. When I asked Sandra, who worked at Pacific Bell during the 1970s and 1980s, what she enjoyed most at her job, she said, "It was the job. I guess we were busier. The timing went so fast and the environment. I really liked it. I liked the job. The whole group, we were like a family in both places." Maria mentioned the "family" structure to me, reflecting on a more complex system of localized information labor. She described the Bell family as "cross-training, and riding with other people, and seeing how other departments work. They exposed everybody to everything so that you pretty much knew what was going on. Everybody was a little bit more considerate. That's what it seemed like. Now the guys don't know what we do, and we don't know who they are. They're badgering us to get it fixed if we could fix it, but it's not like that anymore."[4]

This family structure implied affective pleasure as well as close relationships, two elements these women no longer identified as existing at AT&T or in the larger field of information labor.

Participants used affect to describe their work with information technologies. Recognizing feelings as a mode of agency, these women expressed their work as deeply intertwined with their personal lives. Maria also attributed positive affect to her job, despite the physical toll: "Being physical, I'm glad that I have to climb ladders and walking around. I'm glad I don't have a desk job. It's a wear on my body. I've had several injuries. I just got to be careful and take care of them. I don't regret anything, or being in this same department for so long, three miles from home. I don't mind working. I've always had a nice office."[5]

Maria recalled her forty years at AT&T in conjunction with technological change and the aging process: "Just seeing the technology totally change; I'm looking here in this office and it's half empty. They sent all of the equipment out, and it's not even working, and I don't know where time went. One day I'm like this and the next day I have forty years. I see it all and it's all happening and I'm kind of in denial too. You know, it scares me."[6]

Affect, expressions of joy, anger, displeasure, and pleasure reveal a window into Latina information workers' relationships to telecommunications. Their work with information technologies and lifelong experience of shifting capitalism in the private sector is not contained to office spaces but is messy and intertwined with their domestic lives. For as much as these women analyzed their work in telecommunications as intentionally de-skilled, outsourced, and shifted in a way that does not benefit the information worker, they retained artifacts from their employers. Ann Cvetkovich rethinks the distinction between the public and private spheres: "But as the private life of public culture, the home becomes the soft underbelly of capitalism, a place where the current state of things is experienced through a complex range of feelings" (2012, p. 156). For Latina information workers, these feelings were expressed not only in our interviews but also in their personal collections.

Gloria gathered mementos from GTE (see figure 4.1). Although Gloria's work transitioned through a number of different companies, such as Atlantic Bell and Verizon, Gloria expressed the most sentimental attachment to GTE, a company she saw as paralleling her life story. Gloria's retention of such mementos remembers the days of awards and employment appreciation no longer offered at Bell and Verizon. Monica retained her coffee mug from Pacific Bell and various pins that represented older logos of the Bell system (not pictured). These artifacts denoted another time in telecommunications when the information worker was part of the "family" that many of these women lamented as being long gone. If the home is the soft underbelly of capitalism, the retention of these mementos is a physical manifestation of nostalgia for information work long lost to neoliberal impacts on telecommunications.

Within Latina information workers' oral histories are paradoxes that work with and against this larger narrative of telecommunications and demonstrate its incorporation into their everyday lives and identity narratives. Gloria remembered phone companies as being integral to her own coming-of-age story. She said, "The way I saw my life and where I worked is like we grew up together. You know, General Telephone was probably one of the worst phone companies. It was General Telephone and Pacific Bell, it was only those two, and people had to have you. So, the quality . . . you know what I mean,

Figure 4.1. Gloria's personal collection of awards from GTE

if people have to have you, don't raise the bar. But as things started changing in telecommunications, and General Telephone realizing, 'OK, we're going to change to GTE,' customer service goes up, everything goes up. You have to change. You have to get better if you want to survive."

Belonging and unbelonging to the telephone company, the Bell family, and the larger national family reveals how Latina information workers have been engaged in telecommunications since the

Figure 4.2. Gloria's personal telephone collection

beginning of the *EEOC v. AT&T* consent decree from within the Bell
system and the critical reflections on information technology work
from Latinas at Bell. Latina narratives from below, in information
work limited to blue- and lower-white-collar positions, can offer perspectives into the inner functioning of telecommunications and the
circulation of technologies that may not be available in preexisting
canons. Latina information workers in telecommunications are not
strictly dedicated to telecommunications but also have a personalized

Figure 4.3. Monica's Pacific Bell personal collection

and sometimes contradictory relationship to their work that spills over into their private lives.

The family structure was assigned to Latinas in multiple parts of their lives. The structure was shaped into the Chicano rights movement and therefore shaped the ways in which they received equal rights. It was affirmed in their personal lives as an archetype of "how" Latina/o families should look and function. Latinas entered into a fading family system in telecommunications: the function of that family was once to erode the need for labor unions. They remember that telecommunication familial structure fondly: kinship and a sense of belonging correlated with the preneoliberal company, while detached community relationships and more organized, efficient structures framed their narratives around the neoliberal organizations of telecommunications. Latinas' multiple entrances into "families" shaped their early experiences in information work.

5

THE TELECOMMUNICATIONS LIFE CYCLE

LORRAINE: A CASE STUDY

The final piece of my study centers around Lorraine, a second-generation Mexican American woman from Southern California who has spent most of her life working for the phone company. The goal for this chapter is to focus on one Latina's life in telecommunications as a form of resistance against the larger societal narrative that technology is fueled by sole technological giants—such as Alexander Graham Bell, Theodore Vail, or GTE's Donald C. Power—rather than by many hands. I delve into what Joy Rankin names "the people's history" of telephony: "We need histories not of computers but of the act of computing" (2018, p. 11). Because Latina/os have been historically positioned in technology as blue-collar manufacturers, customer service workers, and occasionally middle management, it is essential that we also document the histories of these positions.

One of my biggest impressions from Lorraine's story is that it is shaped and told by Lorraine herself as a hero's journey. The story has a beginning, where Lorraine enters into the adventure that is her work; a middle, where Lorraine's leadership is challenged by her employees and she must undergo tests; and an end, where Lorraine is laid off after thirty-eight years at the phone company, as Verizon became Frontier.

We see the framing of a hero's journey throughout the history of technology. For example, Mark Zuckerberg's journey to create Facebook amid legal challenges, Steve Jobs building the first Apple computers in his garage, and Alexander Graham Bell patenting the first telephone. The stories about designing and inventing new technologies are framed as tales of single creators who overcame odds to provide the United States with technology that would change users' lives. Lorraine's story reveals that workers at every level of information and technology work have their own hero's journey. My narration is in italics. Because language and voice of marginalized people are important, I keep most of Lorraine's narrative intact as she told it, only changing some language for clarity and using dashes for anonymity.

I call this the *Latina/o telecommunications life cycle* not because it follows one company or the evolution of one technology but because it centers on one Latina/o person's career life span—thirty-six years, in this case. Many of my interview collaborators and their coworkers had worked their entire lives in various forms of AT&T, GTE, Verizon, and more telecom companies. Their identities, embodiments, and memories are the cultural record. They watched businesses change from small independent telephone companies to large corporations; they saw the cord board change into a computerized system. They went from manually entering data into supercomputers to using personal desktops. Their jobs geographically moved over and over again and then would end abruptly. It's not the technology or the corporation that matters in this story line; it is the Latina/o information worker that pulls the string through decades of changes.

ENTERING TELECOMMUNICATIONS

Lorraine was born in Wilmington, California. Lorraine's grandparents were born in Mexico and immigrated early on to the United States, and she is a second-generation Mexican American. Lorraine has lived in Wilmington her entire life. She graduated high school in Wilmington before going on to work at the phone company. Later, Lorraine obtained a business management bachelor's degree from the University of Phoenix, paid for by General Telephone. Lorraine identifies as Mexican, Hispanic,

or Latina. Lorraine's entire life was shaped by telecommunications, tele-
phony, the phone company, and her cultural experience of being Mexican
American in Southern California.

I grew up in Wilmington, California. I graduated from high school and then went back later in life and got my degree in business management. I did a little bit of community college and then I completed my bachelor's with the University of Phoenix. My work paid for it all. It was a nice benefit that a lot of women and men took advantage of. I identify as Mexican, Hispanic, or Latina, and I'm proud of my heritage. I guess probably Latina would be what I would identify as because that's who I am. Things have changed over the years because people would look at you and think, "Where are you from?" Well, I'm darker complexioned too. They would ask, "Are you from India? Or are you Mexican? Spanish?" There were so many other words before the Latina thing came. So now I identify as Latina.

I started working in telecommunications in 1980, right out of high school. That probably goes back to the Latina heritage. My mom didn't really stress education for women. Back then, it was like either go to school or get a job, but it was one or the other, so I was fortunate enough to get in with the phone company. I had an aunt who worked in the phone company, and she said it was a really good job. And at the time, she was already a supervisor, so she said, "There's good opportunities at the phone company for women." So you know, I thought I was pretty smart. I was kind of tired of school, so I said, "OK, I'm going to go and take the test." And then I got hired. I started out as an operator, which is what a lot of us do.

I was hired into GTE as a telephone operator. I was a Traffic Service Position Systems operator. They used to have these machines, and back then they had third-call billing, something called "time and charges." You don't have any of that now, but basically a caller would call in and they would bill to the third party. We would call the third party. So it had to be either a credit card, another phone number, and then I would punch in the number and connect the call. And that's what I did all day. And I loved it because it was just boom, boom. A lot of people start out in directory or as a cord board operator, but what mine was called was a TSPS operator.

I worked as a telephone operator for about twelve months. After six months, you were eligible to transfer. So I stayed about a year, and then I heard I could transfer to another department. I was tired of the hours. One of the greatest things about the phone company were the hours. If you were trying to raise a family or you were trying to go to school or something like that, an operator job was perfect. And later on in my career, I went back to being an operator for that, because they were still flexible. Being younger and stuff, I thought, "Well, you know what?" I wanted to get a little bit closer to home and kind of wanted my hours set a little bit more. So I transferred to the service office, which is what they referred to in those days in Torrance.

So it was called Customer Service Offices, and there was one on Hawthorne Boulevard and Torrance. And that's where I met my best friends Gloria and Nancy, and we've been friends ever since. At that time, we were using a computer with a phone built in. Our dial was called the rotary board. We would all sit around the rotary board, and we would push the button, and everything was on paper. So a customer would call us. We would look up the customer's name on a card. It would have their name, address, the kind of service they had. I did that for about thirteen years.

So we use to use this vacant address file. Any time somebody moved to a new place, you called them up. They were still on the same wheel, but you would look up the papers with their addresses and find out what blocking they had. So eventually they got this computer system called CEBus. That was around 1986.

Everything was still manual, like the billing department. I went to billing, and I was working with microfiche. I was lower in seniority. I was like third on the bottom. So I went to billing, and I used microfiches, and then I also used to do what they called collections. I would get a list of customers who didn't pay their bill. So you would go through this big book, I'm not kidding about big, and you would look up their phone number and you would look to see if they paid their bill. If their bill was still not paid, then it would give you a date and you would call the Temporary Disconnect (TD), and you would disconnect the customer. So I did that job too.

What happened was, the technology was changing, and they started introducing computers and providing training with the phone company. So that was the good thing about the phone company, you know, they provided you the training. They decided to bring all these computers in and consolidated some of the jobs. They asked who wanted to be trained on billing, so I raised my hand. I thought, "Oh, I want to learn this." But when it came time for consolidation, they took everybody that was billing and training and I got relocated to Cerritos, to the billing center. But the people that didn't raise their hand actually got to do more technical work, and I did more administrative.

The phone company had the ability to start introducing computers, so they started doing consolidation. When we had started, everything was in the office from the beginning to end. We handled South Bay, Torrance, then you had another group in Long Beach to do the Long Beach area. So everyone took care of their own area. As they started consolidating, you went in and you started overlapping and taking on other areas. We were right in the midst of all this because we were paper based. In the beginning, you could only take care of a small area.

I was in Cerritos for thirteen years. I went to the billing center, and then I transferred back. So I got forced in line. We were contract employees, and in the contract, there was a line that if we were forced to move, we had the first opportunity to come back in six or seven months when a position opened up. So I came back. I was at the billing center for six or seven months. Then there was a position that opened up and I came back.

I wasn't married before that transfer, and then I got married and was back in Torrance and I had my girls. The company gave me a big baby shower. I was there until 1992 or 1993. I went back and did many different jobs in Control.

There's always a lot of movement because there is a lot of consolidation.

Getting back to the flexibility. After 1992, my friends had gone to other areas. I was pregnant with my son. My daughters were little. Working the 8 a.m. to 5 p.m. was hard because I had to be there. I had twin girls. So I started thinking about transferring, then I got a transfer in 1993. I was pregnant, so it was probably September or October.

I transferred to Long Beach Operator Services. Now, I had never been that kind of operator. That was a "o" operator. But I thought, "You know what, this is going to work for me." Because by then I had more seniority. I could choose the hours I want, it's still close to home. I transferred there. I used to work 4 p.m. to 11 p.m. They use to have these things called short tours. It was 6.5 hours and you got paid for 8. You had breaks and lunch. They called it a short tour because they paid you that extra hour and a half. Anything after 3 p.m. There was another shift if you wanted to. You could work after 11 p.m. for 5.5 hours and get paid for 8. That was GTE. You worked 5.5 hours, you got paid for 8, and got your break and lunch. A lot of mostly women, but some men, took advantage of those hours to go to school and raise their families.

At that time, that was the "o" operator. We used computers and we wore headsets; we talked into the headset, and the call would come into the computer. They were big and simple headsets. I had a girl-friend who use to work 411 operators, and when she started, they had to look up the phone number and address in phone books. They were updated phone books.

I was there for thirteen years and was promoted to management. I had my son and started looking to some of the jobs that were available.

I was promoted for management in 1996. The kids were little. I was making more. As they were getting older, it got easier, and I thought, "Why not? I can do this job." We used to work in the cage where they would monitor us. I was an analyst. My job was to check what time calls would come in. They would foresee the busy times of the "o" operator. I was supposed to take people off and put them online. We had to answer in a certain amount of time. It was on the computer, kind of, but they would give us sheets that we would have to track everything. You use the computer to see who was on calls, but what I was working with was still manual.

So we would say, "At this time we're going to need the computer. We're going to need to add two; we're going to need to minus two." I loved it. I did that job for about three to four years. Then I became a supervisor, and I was a supervisor for the remainder of my time in that office.

From GTE to Verizon

I was a "o" operator when they changed to Verizon.

I loved working for Verizon. I liked GTE too. We were young. It was my first major job. It was like a family. We had people there that would take us by the hand and teach us. When I got pregnant, my ultrasound was passed around the office. You knew your technicians, you knew your customers, you were limited to a specific area.

But technology was changing, phones were changing, so they had to become Verizon. Verizon was a made-up name, by the way. There was no Verizon. GTE merged with the Bells to form a new company.

I was in the Hispanic Support Organization (HSO). They used to put on conferences where we could go, and the company would pay, and we would listen to different types of leadership. When I started hearing and seeing women moving up and going farther within their careers, that's when I went back to school.

I loved being a manager. I had a great boss. The thing about ——— was that I owed him a lot. He called me his number one draft pick. What I learned was my management style. He gave me a chance. There weren't a lot of women in my department—it was me and another woman. There were two women and eight men. But it was a good mix.

In the late 1990s and early 2000s, we started to see more women in the outdoor jobs. So probably in the early 2000s, you had to test, carry a ladder, climb a poll, and a lot of women were intimidated by all that. There were very few, but now I think you probably have more women. There are a lot of women out there now compared to when we started.

When we were becoming supervisors, there were a lot of us women and primarily Hispanics that were moving. We started as operations analysts. There were African American women and Hispanic women that were all getting promoted to supervisor. There were a lot of us that were in the HSO. All of us got promoted. We started as analysts and got promoted to supervisor through the program. I think that had a lot to do with the company promoting the HSO. And ———, who would put our name out there to people that were at her level.

The HSO would teach us elevator speeches. I think primarily, like growing up, my mom did the best she could, but she didn't stress education. We learned that we don't give ourselves kudos. To be modest. We learned a two-minute speech, and we would practice with each other. So I got in an elevator with an executive director, and I said my elevator speech to him, and he said, "Oh, I know who you are."

I wouldn't necessarily be proud of my career, but I think I did pretty good. Once I got into manager, my boss trusted me and he liked my style, that I was a people person. He started giving me work. I had the dispatch center, but I accumulated another work group called CDD, then I got RC Mac, and then, at my peak, I had 176 hourly employees and a staff of about 10. I had four offices. So I was busy. That was again with people that were kind of supporting me, you know, kind of trusting me, supporting me, including my workers and people like Gloria.

Eventually, Lorraine became Gloria's supervisor. When Lorraine began to work with Gloria as her supervisor, the two decided never to talk about work when they spent time together outside of work. As the workplace intensified, offices consolidated and the environment grew more hostile, with one employee targeting Lorraine as a supervisor.

We hadn't worked together in twenty years, so we were getting to work together again. We were really excited. Gloria came to me and said, "You're going to be my manager; we're not going to discuss work." I wouldn't give her information; she wouldn't ask it. We kept it separate. I told my boss, "I have a good friend who is going to be in the workplace," because at that time Verizon was all about diversity and code of conduct. So thank goodness we did this, because years later there would be a woman who would try to report me to Ethics, to say that we were sharing information, taking vacations together. I had to answer questions from Ethics people and from my boss, but we hadn't done anything wrong.

I couldn't tell Gloria what was going on. But someone from Ethics in Chicago called me and interrogated me. They gave me a contract that said that I would agree to move to another job. I said, "No. I've worked too hard for this."

I was gone for like maybe two or three weeks. I can't exactly remember if it was two one-week vacations or two weeks sick or just one and one. So I came back to work. I had to be able to come back to work and hold my head up and be able to, like if they fired me, walk out without crying. And so, I came back, I wrote the thing, I sent it, and I waited and waited to see what happened. And meanwhile, like I said, I couldn't even tell my best friend. I told ——, who was our third party to our friends. She was so mad.

As things were moving along, they wanted to consolidate again. Mission Hills was being sold, so we had to put those people somewhere. There wasn't enough room in Pomona, so they couldn't go there. I had to come up with a place. I didn't want to choose Long Beach because people in Pomona would think I was favoring Long Beach. Pomona didn't have the room. It wasn't cost-effective and it wasn't safe for the women working dispatch late at night; it wasn't in the best area, parking was outside, and it wasn't fenced in. So I took all those things into consideration.

I tried to pick Monrovia because it was central to all three, but Monrovia didn't want the phone company there. In the '70s and '80s, people would go to Monrovia for technology training. Monrovia was a little town, and they didn't want the phone company people there. They liked their little small community. So at that time, Monrovia didn't want us to go there.

I had to work with real estate. I chose Long Beach for several reasons: the freeway was close and in a nice area, enclosed parking, close to the city, and college.

The office was primarily Hispanic and women. They came from Pomona and Whittier.

Then I got promoted to another job after manager, to this program called Black Belt, to provide you training to get certification. It was like a leadership program. I wondered if they wanted me out of the office because of the conflict. That happened in 2014. I went to another job after that. I got to travel to New York a lot.

The Transition from Verizon to Frontier

Lorraine began seeing college graduates coming in and becoming managers. The workplace started changing. New managers and leadership were more hands-off and removed from the physical workplace. Many of the managers were Latina/o and African American women.

The workplace began to prepare to change from Verizon to Frontier.

I was listening in on the transition calls from the Verizon and the Frontier side. Verizon's systems were proprietary, and because they still had offices on the East Coast that were using the same equipment, they wouldn't sell the system and the processes to Frontier. They wanted to use their employees until the cut-over day. They only let Frontier take a handful of people to get trained. So most people weren't trained until the day of the transition. They transitioned from Verizon to Frontier on April 1. I believe it was a Friday, and that Saturday they trained some people, but they literally shut down for a few days to train their people. So the phone company literally shut down for a couple days. So you had employees trying to learn the new system and the new process and equipment that transitioned, so they had outages.

It was a little chaotic for several months. But Verizon didn't allow Frontier to train the employees, and Verizon's records weren't pristine. There were outages. Even today, many employees felt betrayed by Verizon because they sold us out. They wanted to get rid of the wireline business. We were all wirelines. We were all the old school wirelines, and that is a dying business; people don't have old wireline phones. There is still copper out there, but a lot of homes and businesses don't have wirelines.

Verizon was a good company, but you did get kind of lost in it because they were too big. To go from a small mom-and-pop type (GTE) to this huge corporation, it was a lot different. At Frontier, you have to work off a physical spreadsheet. Frontier was a mom-and-pop from the Midwest. They had good intentions, but they just had no idea what they were taking on.

My old department and ——'s department were "seasoned." They learned computers on the job. Some of the people had no knowledge of computers but the ones they worked with. You know we didn't grow up with computers like you all have so they wanted us to be trained. Verizon trained us. They would give you a laptop. The high-tech department needed to hire people off the street because it was high-tech, so they needed to know DSL. So they were younger. They were all from the HSO. They taught you in HSO to be the hand up, to bring people up. So all their employees, they all wanted to help one another. They weren't all Hispanics, but the majority were, and they were like, "We're in this to make us all look good." For a while in older departments, it was survival.

So many people retired when we turned to Frontier because they couldn't keep up. I remember —— used to say, "It takes ten steps to do three steps." You had to know the job but go backward also.

The newer Frontier employees were unionized and younger. The spaces and people were shifting. Workers would come from other offices and merge together into new spaces. The work changed intensely as Verizon shifted to Frontier.

You had to interview for this job and pass the test. The test they had to take was pretty hard and technical. I remember looking at it once, and it was tough. Anytime we got transfers from that office, they were good workers and they were smart. A lot of metrics and focus. Unlike

Verizon, Frontier didn't give you the training. They didn't have the resources. You had to figure it out yourself.

After I left to do the Lane 6 Sigma, it was supposed to be a two-year job for project managing. You're learning how to do different types of jobs. On the East Coast, you would develop an attendance program from like eight different offices and then come up with the best solution with a problem with inadequate record-keeping with attendance, high attendance.

I was short six months of getting my certification, and then Verizon and Frontier merged. For a while, I wasn't sure if I was going to remain Verizon and continue reporting to my boss in New York or become Frontier in California. But part of the merger, Verizon guaranteed Frontier a certain number of employees.

People were leaving quickly during the merger. When they started losing so many people, they made the decision that I would go back to California. Frontier didn't have Lane 6 Sigma, so I came back in February. I saw this really nice man at a meeting, and he was like, "I hear you're coming back. I'll have something for you."

I had a job for a little while in Frontier. I came back in February. We transitioned in April, and my boss in Finance started giving me projects. Frontier looked at it like they "bought" Verizon. I would get a project, I would have to contact people in Frontier, and they thought I was taking their work. They were territorial. So ultimately, my boss and I would lose out. The Frontier legacy person would take over, and I would lose that project.

The Frontier people were intimidated by the Verizon people. There was a lot of chaos. So Frontier decided they weren't going to have any managers. They laid us all off. A thousand of us. So I got laid off. I was one of a thousand. This was in November the year after they merged. The only good thing that happened was that Verizon had this clause that said that if they laid off management people, they would get the Verizon package, which was fifty-six weeks of pay. So it happened before the year was up.

When I look back on it now, it was a good career. For being a woman who didn't have much education, I went back, got an education, was a manager, bought a nice home. I put my kids through college. I got my best friends.

I wasn't bitter. I always told people, "When it's my time, I'm going to step off the train, say it was a good ride, and say it was good while it lasted." If it was five people, if it was because of my performance, I would have felt bad. How could I feel bad when there were a thousand of us let go? They cut out the whole level.

I put in thirty-six years, and I wanted to do forty. It didn't happen, but it was OK. I was lucky to have a long career in one company. Well, three, but the same line of business.

So I got laid off. I had the package and that was going to carry me for a while. I had an aunt that was sick, so I got to spend time with her. My son was graduating from college, so I helped him move to Wisconsin. Then I took the summer off. I had never had the whole summer off. And then here comes the holidays and I said, "I've never had the holidays off. I'll wait for January." So then I said, "I'll start looking February, March."

Lorraine became an independent contractor in engineering at Frontier. There was a new program called "Cap 2" where they took rural areas and running fiber, subsidized by the government. She is uncertain if she'll continue with recontracting. Lorraine feels she can retire even if she doesn't finish her original goal of forty years.

The company is doing good, Fios is doing good, but people are just scrambling to survive. When I look back, my career was good. It was fast. I ran a twenty-four-hour operation. I had my phone on me at all times. We would be on a call sometimes for three or four hours. It was fun. I did it and it was flexible. The majority of the people that worked for me were good. I had a good thing.[1]

CONCLUSION

Why Latinas?

First, and foremost, I seek to make a dent in the field of the history of technology, where Latinas have always been present, invisible, and neglected in the historical record. Without Latinas, a history of technology would not exist. I want to contribute a Latina history of technology for Latinas, with no other purpose than to expand our documented presence in the United States.

As I began my journey into the history of technology and Latina/o studies, I found few published accounts of Latina/os as inventors, creators, users, and hackers. In library and information science (LIS), where I studied and have found my home, Latina/os are overwhelmingly discussed as receivers of information. Receivers of services. Patrons. People to be helped. People to be taught how to use the computer. People who need help setting up an email address.

I stepped back and looked around. *Where are we in the history of creating technology?* I wondered as I positioned myself at the intersection of these unlikely fields. *This picture looks wrong*, I thought as I looked at the mosaic of histories, Latina/o studies, and LIS. I had to look closer. *What do I know? Who is missing?*

My grandfather, Jose, who moved from El Paso to California to work on the railroads and eventually on airplanes. My mom, aunts, and uncles—all of whom worked for phone companies. All of whom began their careers as the consent decree was having an impact, who found stable work at the phone companies. Who moved into the working middle class, with benefits and retirement funds, privileges many independent contractors in this line of work no longer receive. They were the first in their families to work a desktop computer, and they were connecting the lines that made the phones and computers run.

They built and rebuilt communities as their work moved again and again. They migrated around Los Angeles for work as their own parents and grandparents migrated from Mexico to the United States. All navigating their personal lives while swept up in the current of the economic forces creating waves. *We were never not there.* We were never not in the middle of technological development. Every step of the way—for every major technological innovation, from manual to automatic to digital—our bodies were a necessary component for change. Latinas were cast as biologically necessary for the progress of technology and deemed more valuable as invisible to the story of individual innovation.

Latinas have two narratives around technology: the personal and the social. Personally, technology deeply shapes our everyday lives, and for many Latinas in the western United States, technology has been at the center of their work lives as well. They work in the manufacturing, assembly, and customer service roles of technology-based fields. Socially, Latinas have served as the invisible labor by which technology has been produced and delivered, their invisibility an intentional and critical factor to the larger story of innovation, U.S. imperialism, and westward expansion. In telecommunications and at the phone company in particular, Latinas filled a gap in blue-collar labor, their race determined to be flexible depending on accent and phenotype, however not flexible enough to place them in white-collar technology positions in large numbers. The Western narrative of singular White men building technological empires is disrupted by Latina workers, who have long held the wires that made technological invention possible.

Latinas in the United States draw heavily on their personal stories to contextualize their world. The story of a family member who journeyed to the United States to find a better life for their loved ones. The story of the first college graduate in the family. This is part of our story. Latinas are part of the thousands of hands that move voices across continents and borders through the telephones. They have been an essential part of the network of laborers who connected dial-up, broadband, and Wi-Fi. They are the hands that input the data necessary for the phone companies to run efficiently.

The story of Latinas in telecommunications is important, not solely for academic production, or for conference presentations, or for publications. It matters because it matters. Latinas remain heavily underrepresented in the higher echelons of technological fields, but if you pull back the curtain on any area of STEM, you will find that we have always been here. *Latinas on the Line*, then, is a small thread in the fabric that is the Latina/o histories of technology. Latina telephone operators, data entry, customer service, and telephone workers were and are an integral part of the movement of telecommunications, one that brought us from manual to automated to digital.

I establish that Latina/o technological labor has been situated in the early industries of telecommunications. This human labor is the foundation for contemporary digital media and industries built around Silicon Valley and telecommunications companies that presently monopolize the economy. AT&T especially remains a monolith, with deep and long-standing roots. Through the private telephone sector, we see the bridge into privatized access to the internet rather than valuing telephone and internet access as a public good. Latina telecommunications labor is *embedded* into this technological development. Without Latina telecommunications labor, those industries could not have flourished into the technology-centered society that we function in at present. The history of Latina telecommunications labor is the history of labor in the United States, and it must be recognized as such.

The terms of telecommunications are not passively accepted among Latina information workers; they are a dialogue between the employed subject and the larger implemented structures of labor, production, and technological skills. Sites of friction are rationalizations and resistances where Latina information workers negotiate the rapid change in telecommunications. Latina information workers' technological engagements might best be concluded by revisiting a comment that Gloria made to me when I asked her about the constant flux in the telecommunications sector and technology:

> I always . . . umm, *the way I saw my life and where I worked is like we grew up together.* You know . . . umm . . . General Telephone was probably one of the worst phone companies; it was General Telephone and Pacific Bell, it was only those two, and people had

to have you. So the quality . . . you know what I mean if people have to have, you don't raise the bar. But as things started changing in telecommunication, and General Telephone realizing OK we're going to change to GTE. Customer service goes up, everything goes up; You have to change. *You have to get better if you want to survive.*

The frictions in these interviews reveal one of the most important elements of Latina information worker experience: these intimate engagements are identified as the place in which Latinas challenge the larger "story" of telecommunications and technological determinism; they are the place in which the ideology around contemporary capitalism rebuilds itself *and* fails. This research empirically contributes to the historical analysis of Latina labor in telecommunications, but further research on Latina work with information technologies will expand theories of subject formation and resistance in telecommunications, STEM, and IT fields.

Although Latinas were relegated to lower-level information labor, such as telephone operators and data entry, they still engaged in complex analysis of telecommunications, information technologies, and the larger political economy that impacts their everyday labor. Oral history and archival resources are useful tools in extrapolating a labor history yet to be explored. By integrating different disciplines of communications—Latina/o studies, information sciences, and gender and women's studies—histories of Latinas in information technologies could be relevant to multiple fields of thought.

The archives indicate that Latinas were discriminated against through a number of avenues. By the time of the 1973 consent decree, Latinas were generally underrepresented in telecommunications specifically because of nationality, ethnicity, race, gender, and language. During the *EEOC v. AT&T* proceedings, the intersectional needs of women of color were particularly overlooked in favor of solely focusing on gender. MALDEF and CRLA documented a number of discriminations experienced by Latina employees and customers. Latina customers often had to wait long periods of time or did not receive bilingual telephone operator services, finding themselves in emergency situations without the resources to call for help. Latinas in the Bell system were met with a number of discriminations during their employment. Most prominent among the MALDEF and

CRLA reports was the discrimination against Latinas' promotion within AT&T based on their personalities and not their skill set. During their employment by the phone company, Latinas interviewed for this book applied a critical interpretation of both their technological experiences and the larger political economy that framed their work in telecommunications.

The women I interviewed had a deeper commitment to their work when they were using a higher level of skills and given more responsibilities. However, their commitment to telecommunications wavered based on the instability of the political economy, the use of outsourcing, the de-skilling of information labor, and the rapid flux in technology. Such results could contribute to a shift in labor organizing that is relevant to the globalized world. Focusing on the areas in which Latinas challenge the organization of telecommunications and the systems of information labor could strengthen contemporary labor rights movements. Acknowledging that Latina information workers are neither fully dedicated to nor avidly averse to their workplace gives Latinas in telecommunications a nuanced agency that recognizes their complex relations in information technology fields, and capitalism more broadly.

Though many of the women I interviewed spoke Spanish in their personal lives, they did not speak Spanish for or at work, dichotomizing their bilingualism into separate spheres of their daily practices. This trend suggests that Latina information workers who do not speak Spanish for their work also separate their language skills and sociotechno practices, reserving their Spanish fluency for interaction with private domestic technologies.

Increasingly, Latina/os are entering the fields of telecommunications and telephony without unions, with fewer benefits, and with increased dispensability as independent contractors. Because the women interviewed began their work in the early 1970s and 1980s, they are either approaching retirement or currently retired, with sufficient packages to ensure their well-being after their careers have ended. More research is needed on the younger generation that these women have identified.

A critical Latinx technology studies would prioritize Latinas who are from different generational age groups, queer Latinxs, transgender Latinxs, Latinx indigenous politics, Afro-Caribbean Latinas, Black

Latinxs, and Latinxs in the United States without documentation that work in various sectors of STEM fields. Although Latinas are greatly lacking in the thriving tech start-ups and conglomerates of late, especially in management positions, they do indeed work at various levels of skill and information technologies. A critical Latinx technology studies is already happening in the narratives of Latina information workers, who embody intersectional sociotechno practices.

Latinas have always been deep-rooted in U.S. technological development. We must acknowledge that they are members of the invisible information labor sectors that are deemed necessary for technological growth but not important enough to name or credit. The telephone operators, line workers, call center employees, and data entry laborers are part of a vast network that is constantly shifting and is absolutely essential for the maintenance and functioning of the telephone system. Making their stories visible challenges the mythical long-told tales of technological innovators as being individual White males. When expressed, Latinas' lifelong experiences in telecommunications pull back the curtain to reveal an intricate structure of technological development that is reliant on Latina information workers.

ACKNOWLEDGMENTS

I would like to thank the many people that helped me get to this point in my life. Although my name is alone on this book, writing never happens alone and is done with the support of a very strong community.

Thank you to my daughter, Xochitl, for the love, play, and making me a mother. My partner, Julio Cesar, has supported me in every possible way to help me succeed, and I'm so grateful.

Thank you immensely to my parents, Bob and Tina Nicholas, for being so supportive in this long process and always providing me a place to come home to. Thank you to Matt, Candice, and Sofia for embracing me when I come home and providing me space to have fun. Sofia, you have given me so much life and gratitude for every small moment that I spend with you.

This work could never have been completed without the support and safe place that is Joyful Learning Daycare and the excellent staff that always made me feel safe leaving my child with you.

The following sources funded this research: the University of Illinois Urbana-Champaign (UIUC) Gender and Women's Studies Smalley Fellowship, the iSchool at Illinois's funds for doctoral student research travel, the University of Rhode Island (URI) Graduate School of Library and Information Studies (GSLIS) start-up and research funds, URI Faculty Career Enhancement Grant, and URI's Center for the Humanities' Subvention Grant. Thank you to my supportive colleagues at URI's GSLIS. A special thanks to Karen Markin at URI's Division of Research and Economic Development for your expertise and support.

Parts of this book were previously published and have been reprinted with permission from *Media-N*, *Aztlán: A Journal of Chicano Studies*, and *The Intersectional Internet: Race, Sex, Class, and Culture Online*. Thank you to the publishers for permission to reprint.

The Villa and Nicholas families has encouraged my career unconditionally. Thank you so much to my primx Jamie for all of your love and support through this roller coaster that is life. Thank you to my Nina Lynn for taking care of me with laughter and fun! A special thanks to Auntie Teresa, Uncle Mike, Tia Tolly, Uncle Wally, and Uncle John for your expertise and consultation on telecommunications. Thank you for the enthusiasm and encouragement from the Oropeza-Arias family, in California and Irapuato. Thank you to the Villa-Barron family for providing me with a second home throughout my life.

I am so grateful for the friends who picked me up and pushed me through these years. Tracy Drake, Zora, and Aisha Connor-Gaten, you are my home and have saved my life by embracing me over the years; I want to stand in really long Disneyland lines with you. Danielle and Mikah, I owe you more than I can ever give back for welcoming me into your homes and sharing your families with me, I am indebted to Tuesday night wine night with Danielle and discussing superheroes with Mikah while playing with your babies and settling into your couches! Thank you to Jennie and Bethy for your lifelong friendships. Thank you to Kim for taking me out for drinks and always letting me be vulnerable and imperfect. Thank you to Sara and Crystal for providing such wonderful and fun friendships!

Dr. Miriam Sweeney's friendship, time, and constant encouragement have made my career in academia so much better. I'm so grateful to my eternal cohort friends—Dr. LaTesha Velez, Dr. K. R. Roberto, and Dr. Jeanie Austin! You all are so brilliant, and I am honored to have you in my life. Thank you to Berenice, Thomas, Miguel, Tonyia, and Colin for our years at the iSchool at Illinois and for your support and community. Dr. Kathryn La Barre, Dr. Carol Tilley, Dr. Sharon Irish, and Dr. Emily Knox—your activism in the University is greatly admired. A special thanks to Dr. Ethelene Whitmire and Dr. Christine Pawley for your support during my MLS. Thank you to the supportive faculty and staff at the Department of Gender and Women's Studies, including Jacque Kahn and Virginia Swisher for your support and smiles.

Thank you to Dr. Young Lee-Hertig for challenging courses during my undergrad.

Thank you to Dr. Sarah Roberts and Patricia Ciccone, for your support of our family throughout this journey.

Years ago, I walked into Dr. Safiya Noble's office, and she took me in as a student and friend. I know that I'm finishing this book successfully because of her support and encouragement. I am indebted to Dr. Linda C. Smith for your guidance, constant support, and open ears. You have been an example to me of leadership. Thank you to Dr. Angharad Valdivia for your advice and openness to my dissertation and the time you provided through consultation on Latinas in communications; your knowledge and guidance have been indispensable in this process. Thank you to Dr. Sharra Vostral for always being available for questions and advice on my dissertation and career support.

My colleagues at URI GSLIS have been very supportive over the years and have given me a great workplace. I'm so grateful for our excellent office staff Jessica Nalbandian, Cassandra O'Brien, and Jo Knapp. My students have helped me grow over the years in thinking about critical information science. I'm especially grateful to Kathleen Fieffe, Miranda Dube, Kate Fox, and all my students that I constantly see making the field of LIS excellent.

It's impossible to thank all the kind and giving people who have supported this research and process. It takes a whole network of people to finish graduate school and write a book. I appreciate and acknowledge that I could never take sole credit for this project.

NOTES

INTRODUCTION

1. I use the "Bell system" and AT&T interchangeably to refer to the central corporation and their subsidiaries.

2. Monica, personal communication, 2013. All other quotations from Monica come from this interview. All names have been changed.

3. See Venus Green's *Race on the Line* and authors such as Stephen Norwood and Marjorie Stocks.

CHAPTER 1 — WHY LATINAS?

1. More work will be written on the topic of the growth of telecommunications in U.S.-Mexico borderlands and the value of the Latina/o body in technological growth. The full history of Spanish speaking in telecommunications and the increasing demand for a Hispanic independent phone company among advocacy groups is outside of the scope of this study.

2. Between 1879 and 1894, the Bell legal team defended and won six hundred patent infringement suits (John, 2010, p. 203).

3. According to Danielian, public relations included "devices ranging all the way from 'instruction of employees,' and 'public education,' to interference with teaching in schools, editing of school books, buttonholing legislators, patting 'big shots' on the back, and kicking little fellows in softer spots" (Danielian, 1939, p. 271).

4. AT&T would retain its dual identity as a holding company and a network provider until 1984, when a federal judge forced it to sell all its operating companies.

5. AT&T was formed of three different departments: the Commercial Department, responsible for billing, customer services, advertising, and accounting; the

Traffic Department, responsible for telephone service, operator discipline, and training; and the Plant Department, in charge of the construction, installation, and maintenance of line and switchboard equipment (Green, 2001, p. 15). Of these, operators were located in the Traffic Department.

6. The first female telephone operator was Emma M. Nutt, a White woman hired by the New England Bell Company in 1878 (Brooks, 1976, p. 66).

7. From the 1880s on, the multiple switchboard was constantly being upgraded and monitored with new approaches that would increase the operators' workload or decrease the need for operators altogether (John, 2010, p. 237). For a detailed account of switchboard changes, see Venus Green's *Race on the Line*, 2001, pp. 30–46.

8. For an analysis of how the telephone is a gendered instrument, as well as an instrument of gender, see Lisa Rakow's *Gender on the Line*.

9. John asserts that the popularization of the telephone was due to the network expansion of the political economy. State and municipal governments were given authority to regulate the phone company (John, 2010, pp. 270–271). Congress put the telephone and telegraphs under the jurisdiction of the Interstate Commerce Commission (ICC) in 1910. In 1913, Bell and the Justice Department agreed on three provisions in the Kingsbury Commitment: the divestiture between Bell and Western Union, a mandate that Bell could not purchase independent operating companies, and to give independent companies access to Bell's long-distance network (John, 2010, p. 360).

10. Part of this public relations campaign included placing Bell as the socially responsible corporation performing a public service by educating telephone users on the superiority of a telephone monopoly to that of independents and government ownership, see John, 2010, p. 386.

11. In Montana and San Francisco, organizing efforts failed specifically because male union employees as well as feminist groups would not support female telephone operators (Norwood, 1990, pp. 84–87).

12. Bell's own President Vail was known for his condescension and "chivalry" toward women, believing that they should not operate machinery beyond the telephone (Brooks, 1976, p. 147).

13. In lieu of real benefits, Bell would offer "amenities" such as comfortable break rooms, free lunches, tea, and coffee, and company awards. These spaces were also tools of control to keep the operator under the managers' gaze and within the company walls during breaks (Green, 2001, p. 86).

14. Two hundred and twenty-three American women telephone operators worked overseas for the Signal Corps, assisting in establishing a new telephone network in France (Brooks, 1976, p. 156).

15. Operators in particular participated in several strikes across the Pacific Northwest in response to the postmaster general's hostility toward unionism. In New England, strikers gained victories in 1919, which encouraged further national organizing. See Norwood, 1990, p. 158 and p. 208.

16. It should also be noted that this time period saw further technological change, with Alexander Graham Bell making the first coast-to-coast telephone call in 1913, with the invention of a high-vacuum tube used to amplify telephone conversations (Brooks, 1976, p. 139).

17. In 1915, Julia O'Connor became the first WTUL president (Norwood, 1990, p. 121). Labor organizing expanded to the South, West, and Canada (Norwood, 1990, p. 151); though they still did not receive support from the IBEW, they did confront IBEW leadership (Norwood, 1990, p. 152).

18. One exception was the Colorado Telephone Company Benefit Association in Denver, formed in 1906, which created workers' rights specifically based on the needs of women (Green, 2001, p. 108).

19. The dial era lasted from 1920 to 1960. Dial telephones were unpopular to the general public because they were difficult to operate and took away jobs (Green, 2001, p. 160).

20. In 1923, a strike of picketing and unrest ended with the New England Telephone Company dismissing all strikers and replacing them with inexperienced operators (Norwood, 1990, p. 292).

21. Green finds that in such publications as the *Union Telephone Operator* newspaper, Black stereotypes and blackface were used to reinforce White women's superiority in their work (Green, 2001, p. 135).

22. Other sectors included the Plant, Accounting, and Commercial Departments, and not just Traffic.

23. Pacific Telephone and Telegraph specifically ignored Executive Orders 8802 and 9346 (Green, 2001, p. 200).

24. At the 1943 national assembly of the NFTW, members openly discussed how to evade Executive Order 8802, which required integration in the workplace (Green, 2001, p. 207).

25. Unions had a history of excluding Latina/o organizers and members. One such example is the International Ladies' Garment Workers' Union, who refused to support the work of Latina/o organizers after World War II (Vélez-Ibáñez and Sampaio, 2002).

CHAPTER 2 — THE INVISIBLE INFORMATION WORKER

1. Comprised of AT&T and its associate companies.

2. This study uses the term *Latina* to identify women whose cultural, social, and political experiences have often been similar in the United States; however, it resists a narrative that all Latinas might respond the same to their experience as information workers or navigators of information technologies. The use of the term *Latina* is not a neutral or simply descriptive term, but includes a politically engaged debate about the status of Latinas as subjects in the United States.

3. Stockford's account of *EEOC v. AT&T* paints a clear picture between the racial and gendered dichotomies that EEOC oscillated around, but could not

intersect. EEOC attorney David Copus was presented as gender-blind, unconvinced that middle-class women suffered discriminations, while Stockford's protagonist Susan Ross represented and advocated the contemporary White feminist approach in interpreting AT&T discriminations. See Stockford's *The Bellwomen*.

4. Larger structures of race that Carolyn de la Peña names as "at play in all technological production and consumption." De la Peña names Whiteness as a racial epistemology that acts invisibly and goes unnamed in histories of technology (de la Peña, 2010, p. 921).

5. Many scholars have written on this time period as a complete divestment in public services and the move to give private corporations more rights and access to wealth. David Harvey, in the most famous work around neoliberalism, *A Brief History of Neoliberalism*, makes the point that the neoliberal project disembedded capital from the constraints of state-led planning and state ownership, therefore increasing international capitalism as a "utopia project" and reestablishing capitalism as a political project "to restore the power of economic elites." See Harvey, 2011, pp. 11, 19. Lisa Duggan examines the values of the neoliberal project as privatization and personal responsibility. Neoliberalism totes privatization as a critical point of freedom for citizens under capitalism and reaches far beyond the United States, prioritizing the protection of class power and "freedom" to accumulate wealth. See Duggan, 2003, p. 12.

6. Unions were hesitant to get involved, as were EEOC employees. Stockford attributed this to an anti-Black and antiwomen sentiment that had long resonated within unions such as the Communications Workers of America (CWA) and the International Brotherhood of Electrical Workers (IBEW; Wallace, 1976). The unions defended their hesitancy to get involved as representing more than just minorities and women; a win for the EEOC would mean a possible loss of promotions and raises for their White male members. Unions, as a result of decades-old bias, stayed silent and on the sidelines building up to the case. The CWA announced support after *A Unique Competence* hit the media. See Wallace's *Equal Employment Opportunity and the AT&T Case*.

7. The term "Spanish-surnamed Americans" is used throughout *A Unique Competence* to denote Latina/o employees, customers, and potential customers. These numbers may be inadequate in recognizing the actual differentiation among Latina/o employees in the Bell system, considering not all Latina/os have Spanish surnames and those with Spanish surnames may not necessarily be Latina/o.

8. One of the most controversial components of AT&T's hiring practices was their use of psychological tests on selected potential employees. These tests served to systematically stop many underrepresented people from getting

through the job-hiring process and gave AT&T management justifications toward discriminatory practices. The two tests widely distributed were the Wonderlic Personnel Test and the Bennett Test of Mechanical Comprehension. These tests were deemed by the Supreme Court as completely unrelated to job performance yet often engaged to specifically discriminate against Black applicants. A number of aptitude tests and job performance prediction tests were also used adversely to work against Black employment. See Ash, 1976, pp. 203, 208. Bell replaced the Wonderlic with the Bell system Qualification Test I (BSQT I), and on the Wonderlic and BSQT, 70 percent of Whites and 20 percent of Black applicants met the recommended standards. See Lopez, F. (1976). The Bell system's nonmanagement personnel selection strategy. In Wallace, 1976, p. 231.

9. Ethnic organizations such as MALDEF that were involved in the case had deferred to NOW for gender discriminations, having no feminist component of their own. See Green, 2012, p. 48.

10. Asian American experience as employees and customers, prior to and during this case, has yet to be explored deeply within academic scholarship. This research echoes Venus Green's appeal for the investigation into poor women, lesbians, differently abled women, transgender women, and others. See Green, 2012, footnote 17.

CHAPTER 3 — LATINAS ON THE LINE

1. All names have been changed to respect anonymity.

2. Ethnic and race identifiers are used based on how the interview collaborators self-identified.

3. Maria, personal communication, 2014. All other quotations from Maria come from this interview.

4. Gloria, personal communication, 2014. All other quotations from Gloria come from this interview.

5. Sandra, personal communication, 2013. All other quotations from Sandra come from this interview.

CHAPTER 4 — WE WERE FAMILY

1. Chicana feminism emerged during the 1960s and 1970s social movements in an intersectional way that was neglected in mainstream second-wave feminism (usually represented by nonraced White women) and the Chicano movement (usually dominated by Latino men neglecting to consider gender). See Pesquera and Segura, 1998, p. 194. I use the label "Chicana" to indicate a political, race, and gender identity that some Latinas named themselves during these critical years through today.

2. Latinas have a long history of raced, gendered, and sexual subject formations in the United States. Under the gender roles of Spanish colonizing

formation, women in Mexico were held to a binary role of virgin/whore, only allowed to occupy one or the other. Latinas in Southern California in particular inhabited spaces impacted by colonization, land that was once part of Mexico and was indigenous territory before that, resulting in a settler colonial state in which Latinas are often portrayed as foreigners, undocumented, hypersexualized, or hyperreproductive by the mainstream media (Rodríguez, 2003, p. 18).

3. Rodríguez, p. 18.
4. Rodríguez, p. 18.
5. Rodríguez, p. 18.
6. Rodríguez, p. 18.

CHAPTER 5 — THE TELECOMMUNICATIONS LIFE CYCLE

1. Lorraine, personal communication, 2019.

REFERENCES

PUBLISHED SOURCES

Acuña, R., and Compeán, G. (Eds.). (2008). Introduction. In *Voices of the U.S. Latino experience* (pp. xli–lvii). Westport, Conn.: Greenwood.

Amar, P. (2013). *The security archipelago: Human-security states, sexuality politics, and the end of neoliberalism*. Durham, N.C.: Duke University Press.

Anzaldúa, G. (1987). *Borderlands/La frontera: The new mestiza*. San Francisco, Calif.: Aunt Lute Books.

Asencio, M. (Ed.). (2010). *Latina/o sexualities: Probing powers, passions, practices, and policies*. New Brunswick, N.J.: Rutgers University Press.

Ash, P. (1976). The testing issue. In P. A. Wallace (Ed.), *Equal employment opportunity and the AT&T case*. Cambridge, Mass.: MIT Press.

Atske, S., and Perrin, A. (2021, July 16). Home broadband adoption, computer ownership vary by race, ethnicity in the U.S. *Pew Research Center*. https://www.pewresearch.org/fact-tank/2021/07/16/home-broadband-adoption-computer-ownership-vary-by-race-ethnicity-in-the-u-s/.

Báez, J. (2016). Voicing citizenship: Undocumented women and social media. *Chicana/Latina Studies Journal, 6*(1), 56–85.

BBC.com. (2019, December 16). Top tech firms sued over DR Cobalt mining deaths. https://www.bbc.com/news/world-africa-50812616.

Blackwell, M. (2011). *¡Chicana power! Contested histories of feminism in the Chicano movement*. Austin, Tex.: University of Texas Press.

Bohorquez, N. (2014). *Latinas face challenges in STEM*. Technician Online. Accessed February 19, 2015, at https://www.technicianonline.com/arts_entertainment/latinas-face-challenges-in-stem/article_f9d26a2c-745b-11e4-a6d8-2bed14b4212c.html.

Brooks, J. (1976). *Telephone: The first hundred years*. New York, N.Y.: Harper and Row.

Burnett, K., Subramanian, M. M., and Gibson, A. (2009). Latinas cross the IT border: Understanding gender as a boundary object between information worlds. *First Monday*, *14*(9). https://firstmonday.org/ojs/index.php/fm/article/view/2581/2286.

Caballero, C. (2014). *Opinion: Making broadband work for Latinas*. Fox News Latino. Accessed February 23, 2015, at https://www.foxnews.com/opinion/opinion-making-broadband-work-for-all-latinas.amp.

Cantú, N. (2008). *Paths to discovery: Autobiographies from Chicanas with careers in science, mathematics, and engineering*. Los Angeles, Calif.: UCLA Chicano Studies Research Center Press.

Casillas, D. I. (2014). *Sounds of belonging: U.S. Spanish-language radio and public advocacy*. New York, N.Y.: New York University Press.

Cepeda, M. E. (2016). Beyond "filling in the gap": The state and status of Latina/o Feminist Media Studies. *Feminist Media Studies*, *16*(2), 344–360.

Chaar-López, Iván. (2019). Sensing intruders: Race and the automation of border control. *American Quarterly*, *71*(2), 495–518.

Chabram-Dernersesian, A. (1992). I throw punches for my race, but I don't want to be a man: Writing us—Chica-nos (girls, us)/Chicanas—into the movement script. In L. Grossberg, C. Nelson, and P. Treichler (Eds.), *Cultural studies*. New York, N.Y.: Routledge.

Chavez, L. R. (2013). *The Latino threat: Constructing immigrants, citizens, and the nation*. Stanford, Calif.: Stanford University Press.

Cheah, P. (2013). The biopolitics of recognition: Making female subjects of globalization. *Boundary 2*, *40*(2), 81–112.

Collins, P. H. (2001). *Black feminist thought: Knowledge, consciousness, and the politics of empowerment* (2nd ed.). New York, N.Y.: Routledge.

Colón, M. (2002). Line drawing, code switching, and Spanish as second-hand smoke: English-only workplace rules and bilingual employees. *Yale Law & Policy Review*, *20*(1), 227–261. Accessed August 4, 2021, at http://www.jstor.org/stable/41308521.

Cowie, J. (2001). *Capital moves: RCA's seventy-year quest for cheap labor*. New York, N.Y.: New Press.

Crenshaw, K. (1989). *Demarginalizing the intersection of race and sex: A Black feminist critique of antidiscrimination doctrine, feminist theory, and antiracist politics*. Chicago, Ill.: University of Chicago Legal Forum.

Cruz-Janzen, M. (2002). Ethnic identity and racial formation: Race and racism American-style and a lo Latino. In C. G. Vélez-Ibáñez and A. Sampalio (Eds.), *Transnational Latina/o communities: Politics, processes, and cultures*. Lanham, Md.: Rowman and Littlefield.

Cvetkovich, A. (2012). *Depression: A public feeling*. Durham, N.C.: Duke University Press.

Danielian, N. R. (1939). *AT&T: The story of industrial conquest*. New York, N.Y.: Vanguard.

Dávila, A. (2001). *Latinos, Inc.: The marketing and making of a people.* Berkeley, Calif.: University of California Press.

Dávila, A. (2004). *Barrio dreams: Puerto Ricans, Latinos, and the neoliberal city.* Berkeley, Calif.: University of California Press.

de la Peña, C. (2010). The history of technology, the resistance of archives, and the whiteness of race. *Technology and Culture, 51*(4), 919–937.

de Onís, C. (2017). What is an "x"? An exchange about the politics of "Latina/o." *Chiricú Journal: Latina/o Literatures, Arts, and Cultures, 1*(2), 78–91.

Doran, S. (2011). Freedom devices: Neoliberalism, mobile technologies, and governance. In C. McCarthy, H. Greenhalgh-Spencer, and R. Mejia (Eds.), *New times: Making sense of critical/cultural theory in a digital age.* New York, N.Y.: Peter Lang.

Duggan, L. (2003). *The twilight of equality? Neoliberalism, cultural politics, and the attack on democracy.* Boston, Mass.: Beacon.

Encyclopedia Britannica. (n.d.). *GTE Corporation.* Accessed August 5, 2021, at https://www.britannica.com/topic/GTE-Corporation.

Feliú-Mójer, M. I. (2014, November 7). Toward a tipping point for Latinas in STEM. *Scientific American.* https://blogs.scientificamerican.com/voices/toward-a-tipping-point-for-latinas-in-stem/.

Ferguson, R. (2012). *The reorder of things: The university and its pedagogies of minority difference.* Minneapolis, Minn.: University of Minnesota Press.

Fouché, R. (2012). From Black inventors to one laptop per child: Exporting a racial politics of technology. In L. Nakamura and P. A. Chow-White (Eds.), *Race after the internet.* New York, N.Y.: Routledge.

Funk, C., and Parker, K. (2018). *Diversity in the STEM workforce varies widely across jobs.* Pew Research Center. https://www.pewsocialtrends.org/2018/01/09/diversity-in-the-stem-workforce-varies-widely-across-jobs/.

Garcia, F. C. (Ed.). (1997). *Pursuing power: Latinos and the political system.* Notre Dame, Ind.: University of Notre Dame Press.

Garcílazo, J. M. (2016). *Traqueros: Mexican railroad workers in the United States, 1870–1930.* Denton, Tex.: University of North Texas Press.

Gloria Interview. (2014). Interview by M. Villa-Nicholas. [Interview transcript].

Gómez-Peña, G. (2001). *The virtual barrio @ the other frontier: (Or the Chicano interneta).* New York, N.Y.: New York University Press. http://www.pochanostra.com/antes/jazz_pocha2/mainpages/virtual.htm.

Gómez-Quiñones, J. (1994). *Mexican American labor, 1790–1990.* Albuquerque, N. Mex.: University of New Mexico Press.

González, G., and Fernández, R. (1998). Chicano history: Transcending cultural models. In A. Darder and R. D. Torres (Eds.), *The Latino studies reader: Culture, economy, and society.* Malden, Mass.: Blackwell.

Gray, M., and Suri, S. (2019). *Ghost Work: How to stop Silicon Valley from building a new global underclass.* Boston, Mass.: Houghton Mifflin Harcourt.

Green, V. (2001). *Race on the line: Gender, labor, and technology in the Bell system, 1880–1980*. Durham, N.C.: Duke University Press.

Green, V. (2012). Flawed remedies: EEOC, AT&T, and Sears outcomes reconsidered. *Black Women, Gender, and Families*, 6(1), 43–70.

Hall, S. (1990). Cultural identity and diaspora. In J. Rutherford (Ed.), *Identity: Community, culture, difference*. London, U.K.: Lawrence and Wishard.

Hall, S. (1991). Old and new identities, old and new ethnicities. In A. D. King (Ed.), *Culture, globalization, and the world-system: Contemporary conditions for the representation of identity*. Minneapolis, Minn.: University of Minnesota Press.

Harvey, D. (2011). *A brief history of neoliberalism*. Oxford, U.K.: Oxford University Press.

Herr, L. K. (2003). *Women, power, and AT&T: Winning rights in the workplace*. Boston, Mass.: Northeastern University Press.

Hesse-Biber, S., and Carter, G. L. (2000). *Working women in America: Split dreams*. New York, N.Y.: Oxford University Press.

Hicks, M. (2017). *Programmed inequality: How Britain discarded women technologists and lost its edge in computing*. Cambridge, Mass.: MIT Press.

Jackson, M. (2013). *Factsheet: The state of Latinas in the United States*. Center for American Progress. https://www.americanprogress.org/issues/race/report/2013/11/07/79167/fact-sheet-the-state-of-latinas-in-the-united-states/.

Jaschik, S. (2014, November 3). Missing minority Ph.D.s. *Inside Higher Ed*. https://www.insidehighered.com/news/2014/11/03/study-finds-serious-attrition-issues-Black-and-latino-doctoral-students.

John, R. (2010). *Network nation: Inventing American telecommunications*. Cambridge, Mass.: Belknap.

Klor de Alva, J. J. (1998). Aztlán, borinquen, and Hispanic nationalism in the United States. In A. Darder and R. D. Torres (Eds.), *The Latino studies reader: Culture, economy, and society*. Malden, Mass.: Blackwell.

Lopez, F. (1976). The Bell system's non-management personnel selection strategy. In P. A. Wallace (Ed.), *Equal employment opportunity and the AT&T case*, 217–239. Cambridge: MIT Press.

Lorraine Interview. (2019, November). Interview by M. Villa-Nicholas. [Interview Transcript].

MacLean, N. (2006). *Freedom is not enough: The opening of the American workplace*. New York, N.Y.: Russell Sage.

Maria Interview. (2014, August 25). Interview by M. Villa-Nicholas. [Interview transcript].

Martinez, E. (2010, November 2). Chicano librarianship. *American Libraries Magazine*. http://americanlibrariesmagazine.org/features/11022010/chicano-.

Masters, R. S., Smith, R. C., and Winter, W. E. (1927). *A historical review of the San Francisco exchange*. San Francisco, Calif.: Pacific Telephone and Telegraph Company.

McCarthy, C., Greenhalgh-Spencer, H., and Mejia, R. (Eds.). (2011). *New times: Making sense of critical/cultural theory in a digital age.* New York, N.Y.: Peter Lang.

McHenry County Historical Society and Museum. (n.d.). *RR Boxcar Communities.* Accessed August 5, 2021, at https://mchenrycountyhistory.org/rr-boxcar-communities.

Monica Interview. (2013). Interview by M. Villa-Nicholas. [Interview transcript].

Nakamura, L. (2014). Indigenous circuits: Navajo women and the racialization of early electronic manufacture. *American Quarterly, 66*(4), 919–941.

Noble, S. U. (2018). *Algorithms of oppression: How search engines reinforce racism.* New York, N.Y.: New York University Press.

Noe-Bustamante, L., Mora, L., and Hugo Lopez, M. H. (2020, August 11). *About one-in-four U.S. Hispanics have heard of Latinx, but just 3 percent use it.* Pew Research Center. https://www.pewresearch.org/hispanic/2020/08/11/about-one-in-four-u-s-hispanics-have-heard-of-latinx-but-just-3-use-it/.

Northrup, R., and Larson, J. A. (1979). *The impact of the AT&T-EEO consent decree.* Philadelphia, Pa.: Industrial Research Unit, Wharton School.

Norwood, S. H. (1990). *Labor's flaming youth: Telephone operators and worker militancy, 1878–1923.* Urbana, Ill.: University of Illinois Press.

Oboler, S. (2002). The politics of labeling. In C. Vélez-Ibáñez and A. Sampaio (Eds.), *Transnational Latina/o communities: Politics, processes, and cultures.* New York, N.Y.: Rowman and Littlefield.

Ochab, E. U. (2020, January 13). Are these tech companies complicit in human rights abuses of child cobalt miners in Congo? *Forbes.* https://www.forbes.com/sites/ewelinaochab/2020/01/13/are-these-tech-companies-complicit-in-human-rights-abuses-of-child-cobalt-miners-in-congo/?sh=580f2be43b17.

Oropeza, L. (2000). Making history: The Chicano movement. In R. I. Rochin, and D. N. Valdes (Eds.), *Voices of a new Chicana/o history.* East Lansing, Mich.: Michigan State University Press.

Padilla, L. M. (1997). Intersectionality and positionality: Situating women of color in the affirmative action dialogue. *Fordham Law Review, 66*(3), 842–927.

Padios, J. M. (2018). A nation on the line: Call centers as postcolonial predicaments in the Philippines. Durham, N.C.: Duke University Press.

Pesquera, B., and Segura, D. (1998). A Chicana perspective on feminism. In R. Delgado and J. Stefancic (Eds.), *The Latino/a condition: A critical reader.* New York, N.Y.: New York University Press.

Rankin, J. (2018). *A people's history of computing in the United States.* Cambridge, Mass.: Harvard University Press.

Rivin-Nadler, M. (2019, December 22). How ICE uses social media to surveil and arrest immigrants. *Intercept.* https://theintercept.com/2019/12/22/ice-social-media-surveillance/.

Roberts, S. T. (2019). *Behind the screen: Content moderation in the shadows of social media*. New Haven, Conn.: Yale University Press.

Rodriguez, J. M. (2003). *Queer Latinidad: Identity practices, discursive spaces*. New York, N.Y.: New York University Press.

Rodríguez, R. T. (2009). *Next of Kin*. Durham, N.C.: Duke University Press.

Ruiz, V. L., and Sánchez Korrol, V. (2005). *Latina legacies: Identity, biography, and community*. Oxford, U.K.: Oxford University Press.

Sainato, M. (2019, January 1). "We are not robots": Amazon warehouse employees push to unionize. *Guardian*. https://www.theguardian.com/technology/2019/jan/01/amazon-fulfillment-center-warehouse-employees-union-new-york-minnesota.

Saldana-Portillo, M. J. (2007). From the borderlands to the transnational? Critiquing empire in the twenty-first century. In J. Flores and R. Rosaldo (Eds.), *A companion to Latina/o studies*. Malden, Mass.: Blackwell.

Sandra Interview. (2014, August 28). Interview by M. Villa-Nicholas. [Interview transcript].

Santos, F. (2016, September 12). The time I went on a border patrol in a virtual reality world. *New York Times*. https://www.nytimes.com/2016/09/13/us/the-time-i-went-on-border-patrol-in-a-virtual-reality-world.html.

Schaeffer, F. M. (2014). *Love and empire: Cybermarriage and citizenship across the Americas*. New York, N.Y.: New York University Press.

Schiller, D. (2007). *How to think about information*. Urbana, Ill.: University of Illinois Press.

Segura, D. A., and Pesquera, B. M. (1998). Chicana feminisms: Their political context and contemporary feminisms. In A. Darder and R. D. Torres (Eds.), *The Latino studies reader: Culture, economy, and society*. Malden, Mass.: Blackwell.

Segura, D. A., and Zavella, P. (Eds.). (2007). Introduction. In *Women and migration in the U.S.-Mexico borderlands*. Durham, N.C.: Duke University Press.

Sinclair, B. (2004). *Technology and the African American experience: Needs and opportunities for study*. Cambridge, Mass.: MIT Press.

Sohail, U. (2020, February 20). This is a story of life and death in Apple's forbidden city you never heard of. Wonderful Engineering. https://wonderfulengineering.com/story-life-death-apple-forbidden-city/.

Stockford, M. A. (2004). *The Bellwomen: The story of the landmark AT&T sex discrimination case*. New Brunswick, N.J.: Rutgers University Press.

Sweeney, M., and Villa-Nicholas, M. (2022). Digitizing the "ideal" Latina information worker. *American Quarterly*.

Torres, C. A. (2019, September 17). Tourists are flocking to this tiny mountain village for a trip on Mexico's magic mushroom. *Mitú*. https://wearemitu.com/culture/what-you-need-to-know-about-the-magic-mushroom-tourism-craze-in-oaxaca/.

Tsing, A. L. (2005). *Friction: An ethnography of global connection*. Princeton, N.J.: Princeton University Press.

Tunstall, W. B. (1985). *Disconnecting parties: Managing the Bell system break-up, an inside view.* New York, N.Y.: McGraw-Hill.

U.S. Department of Education. (2014). *Hispanics and STEM Education.* https://www2.ed.gov/about/inits/list/hispanic-initiative/stem-factsheet.pdf.

Valdivia, A. N. (2018). Intersectional borders: A challenge to the field of communication and media studies. In A. Shaw, and D. T. Scott (Eds.), *Interventions: Communication research and practice* (pp. 85–94). New York, N.Y.: Peter Lang.

Vélez-Ibáñez, C. G., and Sampaio, A. (Eds.). (2002). *Transnational Latina/o communities: Politics, processes, and cultures.* Lanham, Md.: Rowman and Littlefield.

Vigil, M. (2000). The ethnic organization as an instrument of political and social change: MALDEF, a case study. In M. Gonzales and C. M. Gonzalez (Eds.), *En aquel entonces: Readings in Mexican American history.* Bloomington, Ind.: Indiana University Press.

Villa-Nicholas, M. (2014). Latina narratives of information technologies: Towards a critical Latina technology studies. *Media-N, 10*(3). http://median.newmediacaucus.org/art-infrastructures-information/latina-narratives-of-information-technologies-towards-a-critical-latina-technology-studies/.

Villa-Nicholas, M. (2015). Latina/o librarian technological engagements: REFORMA in the digital age. *Latino Studies, 13*(4), 542–560.

Villa-Nicholas, M. (2016). Ruptures in telecommunications: Latina and Latino information workers in Southern California. *Aztlán: A Journal of Chicano Studies, 42*(1), 73–97.

Villa-Nicholas, M., and Sweeney, M. (2020). Designing the "good citizen" through Latina identity in USCIS's virtual assistant "Emma." *Feminist Media Studies, 20*(7), 909–925.

Villa-Nicholas, M. (2019) Latinx Digital Memory: Identity Making in Real Time. *Social Media and Society, 5*(4).

Villa-Nicholas, M. (2020). Data body milieu: The Latinx immigrant at the center of technological development. *Feminist Media Studies, 20*(2), 300–304.

Wajcman, J. (2009). Feminist theories of technology. *Cambridge Journal of Economics, 34*(1), 143–152.

Wallace, P. A. (Ed.). (1976). *Equal employment opportunity and the AT&T case.* Cambridge, Mass.: MIT Press.

Wallace, P. A., and Nelson, J. E. (1976). Legal processes and strategies of intervention. In P. A. Wallace (Ed.), *Equal employment opportunity and the AT&T case.* Cambridge, Mass.: MIT Press.

Wallis, C. (2013). *Technomobility in China: Young migrant women and mobile phones.* New York, N.Y.: New York University Press.

Wilson, R. H., and Teske, P. E. (1990). Telecommunications and economic development: The state and local role. *Economic Development Quarterly, 4*(2), 158–174.

Winner, L. (1986). *The whale and the reactor: A search for limits in an age of high technology.* Chicago, Ill.: University of Chicago Press.

Wu, T. (2011). *The master switch: The rise and fall of information empires*. New York, N.Y.: Vintage.

Zuckerman, E. (2008). *Beyond dispute:* EEOC v. Sears *and the politics of gender, class, and affirmative action, 1968–1986* [Doctoral Dissertation, Rutgers University, New Brunswick]. Rutgers University Library Commons: https://rucore.libraries.rutgers.edu/rutgers-lib/25073/.

ARCHIVAL SOURCES

Alvarado, M. (1972). "An Attitudinal Survey: Alameda County Survey of Mexican-American Subscribers, and Potential Subscribers, to Pacific Telephone and Telegraph Services." Mexican American Legal Defense and Education Fund Records. M0673, Box 653, Folder 3. Stanford University Libraries. Department of Special Collections and University Archives.

California Rural Legal Assistance Records. (ca. 1971). Anne Hay case no. 491. Box 1251, Folder 3. Stanford University Libraries. Department of Special Collections and University Archives.

California Rural Legal Assistance Records. (ca. 1971). Letter to Ann Hille. Box 967, Folder 5. Stanford University Libraries. Department of Special Collections and University Archives.

California Rural Legal Assistance Records. (1971). Box 1251, Folder 2. Stanford University Libraries. Department of Special Collections and University Archives.

California Rural Legal Assistance Records. (1979). Box 1251, Folder 5. Stanford University Libraries. Department of Special Collections and University Archives.

California Rural Legal Assistance Records. (1980a). Letter to Ben W. Dial. Box 48, Folder 3. Stanford University Libraries. Department of Special Collections and University Archives.

California Rural Legal Assistance Records. (1980b). Pacific Telephone's 1972 Commitment of Employment of Hispanics. Box 47, Folder 2. Stanford University Libraries. Department of Special Collections and University Archives.

Evangelista, M., and Gonzales, J. (1975). List of definitive questions to Pacific Telephone. AT&T Consent Decree. Mexican American Legal Defense and Education Fund Records. Box 653. Stanford University Libraries. Department of Special Collections and University Archives.

Hamilton, Susan. (1975, June 18). AT&T Consent Decree. Mexican American Legal Defense and Education Fund Records. Box 653. Stanford University Libraries. Department of Special Collections and University Archives.

Mexican American Legal Defense and Education Fund Records. (1972a). Witnesses, M0673. Box 652. Stanford University Libraries. Department of Special Collections and University Archives.

Mexican American Legal Defense and Education Fund Records. (1972b). Witnesses, M0673. Box 653. Stanford University Libraries. Department of Special Collections and University Archives.

Mexican American Legal Defense and Education Fund Records. (1972c). Witnesses, M0673. Box 655. Stanford University Libraries. Department of Special Collections and University Archives.

Mexican American Legal Defense and Education Fund Records. (1975). Box 653, Folder 9. Stanford University Libraries. Department of Special Collections and University Archives.

Papers of Marjorie Stockford. (ca. 1972). Consent decree. Civil Rights Litigation Clearinghouse, EE-PA-0227–0001. University of Michigan Law School. Ann Arbor, Michigan. Accessed at http://www.clearinghouse.net/detail.php?id=11146.

Papers of Marjorie Stockford. (1972). *A unique competence: A study of equal employment opportunity* (as reprinted in the Congressional Record). E1267. Civil Rights Litigation Clearinghouse. University of Michigan Law School.

Papers of Marjorie Stockford. (ca. 1974–1979). Copus, D., Gartner, L., Speck, R., Wallace, W. Feagan, M., and Mazzaferri, K. *A unique competence: A study of equal employment opportunity*. Civil Rights Litigation Clearinghouse, EE-PA-0227–0003. University of Michigan Law School. Ann Arbor, Michigan. Accessed at http://www.clearinghouse.net/detail.php?id=11146.

Papers of Marjorie Stockford. (ca. 1974-1979). Copus, D., Gartner, L., Speck, R., Wallace, W., F. M., and Mazzaferri, K. *A unique competence: A study of equal employment opportunity congressional record*. Civil Rights Litigation Clearinghouse, EE-PA-0227–0004. University of Michigan Law School. Ann Arbor, Michigan. Accessed at http://www.clearinghouse.net/detail.php?id=11146.

New York Telephone Company. (1917). *The telephone review*. New York, N.Y.: New York Telephone Company.

INDEX

Page numbers followed by *t* refer to tables.

ABOUT THE AUTHOR

MELISSA VILLA-NICHOLAS is an assistant professor at Harrington School of Media and Communications' Graduate School of Library and Information Studies at the University of Rhode Island. Her research interests include the history of Latinxs with information technologies and within information spaces, Latinx science and technology studies, and critical information science. Her publications include "Data Body Milieu: The Latinx Immigrant at the Center of Technological Development" in *Feminist Media Studies* and "Missing Cells: The Growing Economic Value of Immigrant and Refugee Biological Data" on Bitch Media.